Wealth

Richard P. Rojeck

Wealth

The Ultra-High Net Worth Guide to Growing and Protecting Assets

palgrave
macmillan

Richard P. Rojeck
La Jolla, CA, USA

ISBN 978-3-030-24499-6   ISBN 978-3-030-24497-2   (eBook)
https://doi.org/10.1007/978-3-030-24497-2

© The Editor(s) (if applicable) and The Author(s), under exclusive license to Springer Nature Switzerland AG, part of Springer Nature 2019
This work is subject to copyright. All rights are solely and exclusively licensed by the Publisher, whether the whole or part of the material is concerned, specifically the rights of translation, reprinting, reuse of illustrations, recitation, broadcasting, reproduction on microfilms or in any other physical way, and transmission or information storage and retrieval, electronic adaptation, computer software, or by similar or dissimilar methodology now known or hereafter developed.
The use of general descriptive names, registered names, trademarks, service marks, etc. in this publication does not imply, even in the absence of a specific statement, that such names are exempt from the relevant protective laws and regulations and therefore free for general use.
The publisher, the authors and the editors are safe to assume that the advice and information in this book are believed to be true and accurate at the date of publication. Neither the publisher nor the authors or the editors give a warranty, expressed or implied, with respect to the material contained herein or for any errors or omissions that may have been made. The publisher remains neutral with regard to jurisdictional claims in published maps and institutional affiliations.

Cover image: © Jun/iStock/Getty Images Plus

This Palgrave Macmillan imprint is published by the registered company Springer Nature Switzerland AG
The registered company address is: Gewerbestrasse 11, 6330 Cham, Switzerland

Preface

This book is written for the wealthy. About that I make no apologies. Definitions of wealthy and related terms such as ultra high net worth or super affluent are as numerous as those who offer them. Labels notwithstanding, these are individuals who have achieved exceptional levels of personal and financial success. And they have contributed significantly to our economy, and often, society as a whole. They also share the distinction of being amongst the top 1% of income earners who will pay over 40% of the federal individual income tax.[1] And they will certainly be in the .2% of Americans whose estates, collectively, are destined to pay an estate tax.[2] Depending upon the direction of the political winds, their tax burden could rise even further. These and other factors give credence to the saying that, "It's easier to make money than to keep it."

This group, while hotly pursued by purveyors of financial advice, in many ways, is underserved. Almost without exception they have retained the services of capable advisors: attorneys, CPA's, investment bankers, trust officers, investment advisors, and insurance experts. And they have assembled many of the components of a financial plan: wills, trusts, business agreements, investment portfolios, and insurance. But these disparate components were implemented at different times, with different advisors, with differing perspectives, are often uncoordinated and often out of date. Frustration by an inability to gain clarity or simply to bring "closure" to their planning is not uncommon.

---

[1]Source: Tax Policy Center; Urban Institute & Brookings Institution, 2017.
[2]Source: Joint Committee on Taxation, US Congress.

This book stands for the proposition that the best defense against high and rising income and estate taxes and other threats to your wealth emerges from a comprehensive, integrative process, guided by a qualified financial planner. Such an individual will help you see the big picture, help you identify your values and goals, and then work with you to identify and assemble the specific components to best achieve those values and goals and defend your hard-earned wealth. Integral to the process is the creation of a financial model which will be indispensable in evaluating present and forecasting future outcomes. Working with your other advisors, he or she will ensure the plan is coordinated, implemented and updated.

Our journey will cover eight topics in as many chapters. As we visit each I suspect you will read about some strategies with which you are familiar and perhaps which you have already implemented. I also suspect you'll learn about many others of which you weren't aware. I will urge you to consider each in the context of your values and goals and of course how they can be best evaluated through a financial planning process. Chapter 9 addresses the subject of how to select a qualified financial planner. And in Chapter 10 I attempt to draw it all together through a series of questions which I hope you'll find thought-provoking. For the Type A personalities, you may wish to skip to Chapter 10, then work backwards to the corresponding chapters (just don't skip any!).

Let's get started.

La Jolla, USA   Richard P. Rojeck

Acknowledgements

It's been said "everyone has a book in them" (with variations including "and in most cases, that's where it should stay"). Seldom mentioned is the gestation and labor process associated with giving birth to it. There are a number of individuals to whom I am grateful for their assistance in the process. Foremost is my niece Danielle Paghorian whose nickname "Starr" is an apt description of her contributions in research and typing (and re-typing as the whimsy of my word selection often required). My administrative assistant, Ashley Green Altick, added the finishing touches. Paul Robinson, PhD, contributed a professorial review for syntax and punctuation. And Mark Russell performed a remarkably painless compliance review. I am also indebted to the many who provided a technical review (while I reserve full credit for any remaining inaccuracies or deficiencies): Nasser Ali, CFP®, CFA, Bob Appel, J.D., LL.M., Paul Dostart, J.D., LL.M., Ben Huddle, CFP®, Tim Johnson, J.D., and Ken Weiss, C.P.A., J.D., LL.M. Finally, I'd like to thank the most important people in my life, Joji, my wife and best friend of 41 years and the joy of our lives, our three children, Jessica, Alexandra and Jason. You make it all worthwhile.

Contents

List of Figures

List of Tables

1

Wealth

In his book, The Affluent Society, American economist John Kenneth Galbraith writes "Wealth is not without its advantages and the case to the contrary, although it has often been made, has never proved widely persuasive."[1] The creation and accumulation of wealth being the natural outcome of an ambitious individual encountering a free-market system, the question remains only "how much wealth is enough?" At the individual level, the answer to "Do I have enough?" can be both a mathematical as well as an emotional issue, and it has very little to do with the traditional notion of retirement. The question, "Do I have enough?" can be translated into "Am I financially independent?"

Of course the answer depends on your desired lifestyle, since we know that there is no amount of wealth that a given standard of living could not consume. People with vast sums of wealth are declaring personal bankruptcy merely because of an out-of-control lifestyle.

The answer also depends on how you define your financial independence, for which I suggest the following definition: "Being able to enjoy one's desired standard of living while engaging in one's desired activities, without regard to the current rewards associated with them." In other words, "I want to be able to do what I want to do when I want to do it and not care about the financial rewards."

As you think about financial independence, it's important that you consider whether it should be built on the endowment or the annuity concept.

---

[1] John Kenneth Galbraith, *The Affluent Society* (Boston: Houghton Mifflin, 1958).

© The Author(s) 2019
R. P. Rojeck, *Wealth*,
https://doi.org/10.1007/978-3-030-24497-2_1

Let me explain. An endowment is a sum of money sufficient in amount such that the earnings (current income plus appreciation) are sufficient to provide for the need, adjusted for inflation, forever. In other words, your original capital will remain intact and, in fact, will grow at least at the rate of inflation. The point in building an endowment is so you never have to worry about how long you live. Life expectancy becomes irrelevant. I would suggest this is the truest measure of financial independence. And, by definition, at your death, your wealth will pass to your heirs and or to society.

By the Numbers

You have heard about college endowments or endowments for the arts. This is the same concept. The amount of the endowment is deemed sufficient to pay for a college professor's salary, or to augment an opera's performing costs, or an art museum's operations, indefinitely, without consuming the original principal, adjusted for inflation. The process starts by establishing an expected long-term return for its investment portfolio: 7–8% is most common. From this is subtracted the expected rate of inflation, the portion of the return that must be reinvested, to allow the portfolio to grow and offset the future impact of inflation. The U.S. inflation rate has averaged about 3% over the past 100 years. Subtracting 3% from 7% yields the 4% spendable return commonly used. As charities are generally tax exempt, absent from this calculation is an adjustment for income tax. So for example, an endowment of $2.5 million invested at 4% net, would generate income of $100,000 annually to support the organization's operations.

The annuity concept, on the other hand, assumes that a sum of capital is accumulated so that—based upon an anticipated investment return—the principal plus earnings on a declining balance will satisfy the need for a given period of time. In this case, the given period of time is, of course, how long you plan to live. In other words, in addition to consuming all the income, you are also using up an increasing amount of the principal each year until it is exhausted.

The risk here is that you may live too long, exhaust your principal, and wind up on your children's doorstep, tin cup in hand. Given the choice, most everyone would prefer the endowment approach. But like everything else in life, you get what you pay for. Endowment "costs" more, and therefore, has implications on everything else, from how long you must work, how much you must sacrifice in order to save, your future sustainable income, and everything in-between.

Let's look at an example, first taking the endowment approach. Assume your desired lifestyle comes with a $1 million annual price tag after tax, meaning you spend about $83,000 per month. If we use 3% as the assumed after-tax investment return (versus 4% in the case of a tax-exempt organization), dividing $1 million by 3% yields required invested capital of $33.3 million. Of course, invested capital excludes your other, non-income-producing assets such as your home, a second home, furnishings, artwork, cars, a yacht, etc. In contrast the annuity approach would require just $21 million using the same assumptions and a 30-year life expectancy. Results are proportional, so if your lifestyle is $2 million, $3 million or more, simply increase the required sums accordingly.

The mathematics behind this endowment approach is similar to that in valuing income-producing assets, whether they be bonds, oil wells, stocks, real estate, or closely held businesses. The income stream (e.g., interest, dividends, net operating income) is divided by a discount or "cap rate" to yield a "present value" or today's dollar equivalent of the income stream, which yields the price a buyer would pay to acquire it. So in our example above, a buyer would be willing to pay $33 million in order to purchase a $1 million income stream, after tax, paid indefinitely, adjusted for inflation.

While this methodology is broadly accepted and, arguably, straightforward, it does have a shortcoming in that it assumes a consistent investment return. That is, it assumes the investment portfolio earns 7%, inflation is 3%, taxes 1%, every year. But we know this is not the case; investment returns can vary widely from year to year and this can have a big impact on the outcome. In fact a significant body of research supports the notion that the pattern or sequence of returns greatly influences whether your assets will be sufficient to sustain your lifestyle.[2]

To more accurately determine the amount of invested capital necessary, considering the variability of returns, financial planners often use a Monte Carlo simulation. It gets its name from the famous Mediterranean seaside resort known for its casinos and high rollers. Monte Carlo simulation seeks to determine the likelihood of a given outcome by running numerous trials or iterations, typically 1000. It's particularly useful when no mathematical formula exists to precisely calculate an outcome, though as a simulation, the result is a range of outcomes rather than a precise forecast.

---

[2]Philip L. Cooley, Carl M. Hubbard, and Daniel T. Walz, "Portfolio Success Rates: Where to Draw the Line," *Journal of Financial Planning* 24, no. 4 (April 2011): 48–60.

Let's look at a Monte Carlo simulation outcome for our example: $1 million lifestyle, 3% inflation assumption and 7% annual returns from a broadly diversified portfolio. For a $50 million investment portfolio, there would be virtually a zero percent probability of portfolio depletion, 62% probability of preservation of the original sum, with a $66 million median ending balance (i.e., half the outcomes were above and half were below this sum), adjusted for inflation in 30 years. Obviously, this tool can provide valuable insight.

Another way to forecast financial independence is to simply use a spreadsheet, conservatively projecting income from existing businesses, real estate, your investment portfolio and other holdings, considering income tax and the impact of inflation on the income need.

Enough Already

Enough about the mathematical implications, what about the emotional dimensions of "Do I have enough?" People are motivated by a variety of factors: fear, greed, guilt, altruism, competitiveness—any of which may drive them to aspire to and strive for a certain level of wealth. Often, these attitudes and values were imparted by parents or influential figures or developed through life experiences. They can be both constructive and destructive. Discerning the difference and knowing when you have "enough" can be an enlightening experience.

We're all familiar with the concept of diminishing marginal utility. Thinking about the marginal utility of nice to haves: a bigger or a second or third home, a yacht, or airplane and whether they bring you genuine happiness, may help you answer the question "Do I have enough?" There are, after all, consequences associated with acquiring and maintaining them: the potential toll on your financial security, your health, family and other relationships. Understanding the trade-offs frees you to put less at risk (Fig. 1.1).

I'm reminded of a client who was very nearly financially independent, enjoying a seven-figure lifestyle and an eight-figure estate built as a real estate developer and investor. He was neither liquid nor well-diversified. And he was highly leveraged, convinced it would support even greater wealth accumulation. When I challenged him with the question, "Is it really necessary to put so much at risk in the pursuit of more?", he was dismissive of the notion that he was overly aggressive. The year was 2007. In the ensuing financial crisis his assets fell like dominos and he found himself having

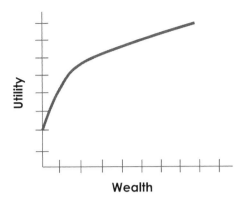

Fig. 1.1 Utility of wealth

to virtually start over. Perhaps a check on your own situation is to ask yourself, "In the next financial crisis, will I be a *buyer* of distressed assets, or a *seller* of them?"

Of course, many continue to build wealth not from a need to secure financial independence. They are financially independent many times over, living comfortably, well within their means. They enjoy their worldly possessions but are not enslaved by a need for more of them. They love the occupation by which they've earned their wealth, and are exceptionally good at it. And so their estate continues to grow.

It's been said, "You're rich when you know you have enough." A financial planner can be the catalyst to helping you determine what's important and where your utility function begins to diminish and the curve flattens. She can do the modeling to help you quantify "enough." And she can show you how to deploy surplus wealth for the benefit of your family and community.

Questions to Consider

- Do you have enough?
- Do you have adequate liquidity and reasonable diversification?
- Is your debt level and structure prudent considering the risk to your financial security?
- Do you have a plan to deploy your surplus wealth for the benefit of your family and community?

2

Estate Planning

The only truly dead are those who have been forgotten.

—Jewish proverb

For many, the thought of planning one's estate is about as enticing as a root canal. Estate planning involves confronting one's mortality: that we won't live forever and that our demise from any number of causes—accident or illness—could come suddenly upon us. Nonetheless it is a fundamental part of the financial planning process.

Estate planning basically entails the arrangement of your affairs to ensure that your worldly assets pass to whom you want, when you want, and in the proper portion. Ideally that distribution will be unencumbered by the cost, delays, and publicity involved in the probate process. It also addresses the potentiality of your needing assistance in managing your affairs during your lifetime, should you become incompetent to do so, due to advanced age or illness. This includes specifying the medical care you desire and who shall make those decisions on your behalf. Finally, the estate plan should serve to reduce, if not eliminate, the impact of federal and state estate and inheritance taxes.

The challenge in estate planning for high net worth individuals is principally three-fold:

- Defining a legacy—what you want to leave behind for your family and society
- Establishing an infrastructure in support of the legacy, including family governance
- Dealing with a potentially significant transfer tax.

© The Author(s) 2019
R. P. Rojeck, *Wealth*,
https://doi.org/10.1007/978-3-030-24497-2_2

Shirtsleeves to Shirtsleeves

There's an old expression, which actually exists in many societies, reflecting its universal truth: "Shirtsleeves to shirtsleeves in three generations." This refers to the phenomenon of wealth being created by the first generation, enjoyed by a privileged, but unproductive, second generation, and often exhausted by the third. Often contributing to this outcome is an estate design which provides for segregation of assets into separate shares for each child, with outright distribution in increments (e.g., ages 30, 40, and 50). A variation is that certain assets are held through the child's lifetime and then distributed to grandchildren in the same fashion. For a family with three children and six grandchildren, the estate is split three ways (after applicable estate tax) and at the children's level (after applicable estate tax) split six ways and ultimately distributed outright to the grandchildren. All the while beneficiaries have received trust distributions regardless of their need, individual productivity, or other considerations. The following diagram depicts such a plan (Fig. 2.1).

There is another approach. It starts with attempting to determine how much wealth is enough. Warren Buffett was quoted as saying the perfect amount of money to leave children is "enough money, so they feel they could do anything, but not so much so they could do nothing." It involves identifying the values you hold dear, have no doubt been attempting to instill in your children and perhaps grandchildren, and wish to continue reinforcing. They might include self-determination, self-reliance, hard work, pursuit of higher education/lifetime learning, entrepreneurship, leadership, charity, and others.

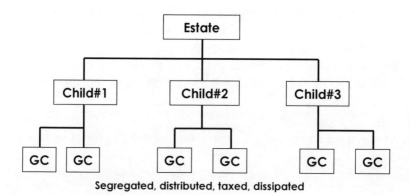

Segregated, distributed, taxed, dissipated

Fig. 2.1 Typical estate plan

Importantly, it often involves wealth concentration, holding assets together rather than segregation and ultimate distribution as described above. It could entail the creation of a family trust, often referred to as a family "bank," intended to last for many generations from which distributions are made in support of those values. Such distributions include college and post-graduate education (possibly including stipulation of a minimum GPA and completion date). They may also include a distribution or loan for purchase of a first home, or a loan for investment in a business (on favorable terms but predicated on an accepted business plan). Distributions could also be made for medical insurance premium payments or uninsured medical expenses or a disability and perhaps income upon attainment of a specified retirement age. But they do not include distributions that may only serve to support an early retirement or profligacy. The goal of such a trust is to transfer incentives and opportunities, not just wealth. Through proper planning it is possible to have a positive impact on the lives of your children, grandchildren, and future generations.

Trusts benefiting two, three, or more generations last 100 years or more. So it must be realized that wealth preservation is a business, regardless of whether family assets actually consist of a business. The key to success lies in family governance.

Planning for Success

If it were as simple as having a well-designed multi-generation trust, what then accounts for the phenomenon that an estimated 70% of wealth transfer plans are unsuccessful: family unity and cohesion is not maintained following the death of the parents. The causes have been attributed to the following[1]:

60% Trust and Communication Breakdown
25% Failure to Prepare Heirs
10% No Family Mission
5% All Other

A not uncommon scenario is the highly successful entrepreneur or corporate CEO whose singular focus and drive in pursuit of his career results in

---

[1]Roy O. Williams and Amy A. Castro, *Bridging Generations—Transitioning Family Wealth and Values for a Sustainable Legacy* (Oviedo, FL: HigherLife Developmental Services, 2017), 6.

his amassing significant wealth, often at the expense of family relationships. Despite an affluent upbringing, the children often do not share the same values and goals as the generation from which their parents come. Controlling by nature, wealthy parents feel they deserve to transfer their wealth as they see fit, without a great deal of collaboration with and input from their children and grandchildren, who in fact would welcome such interaction. The seeds are thus sown for an unsustainable and unsuccessful multigenerational estate plan.

To put this in clearer perspective, let's take a look at the elements of a sophisticated estate plan, and how they might backfire with ill-prepared beneficiaries. The estate plan provides that assets are held in trust in lieu of outright distribution in order to provide asset protection and estate tax relief for future generations. But the children ask "why did they tie up the assets, giving us no direct access?" The trust provides no regular distributions, but instead supports opportunities such as education, a first time home purchase, or seed capital for a business. And the children wonder, "They had so much, why can't I get a regular check?" The trust encourages participation on an investment committee or as co-trustee. Yet the children feel they had no preparation or training or even interest in doing so.

The remedy for this, of course, is to recognize first and foremost that family wealth doesn't consist merely of financial assets: stocks, bonds, real estate and closely-held businesses. It also consists of "the family itself, including its history, experience, and education; the intellectual, social, and networking capacity of all family members, including spouses; and most importantly, the existing asset of the entire family itself, children and spouses, grandchildren…and the family values, unity and harmony."[2]

A starting point in the preparation process would be a discussion of family values. An effective means of identifying and articulating shared values within a family is through the creation of a family mission statement. It can also express a shared dream or vision for the family and its members. In *Complete Family Wealth*, the authors state that a thoughtful family mission statement should address the following questions[3]:

* What are our core values as a family?
* Why do we want to stay together as a family?

[2]Ibid., 2.

[3]James E. Hughes, Jr., Susan E. Massenzio, and Keith Whitaker, *Complete Family Wealth* (Hoboken, NJ: Wiley, 2018), 138.

- What family traditions do we want to preserve?
- What impact do we as a family want to have on the world?
- How much do we want to be connected and how much do we want to be independent?

The creation of a family mission statement, while certainly influenced by the senior generation through its parenting, mentoring and family enterprise management, is nonetheless best developed with the input of the entire adult family. Family meetings are a good format for this type of work. A family retreat at a conference or resort facility involving a professional family wealth coach is often helpful and, for some families, vital. This is a process which, given adequate time and effort, can produce a powerful outcome—guiding the family business, philanthropy and of course estate planning arrangements for the benefit of present and future generations.

Preparation for future roles is an ongoing process, whether it be in entering the family business, involvement with determining grants from the family's private foundation or participating in investment management. Of course, all such involvement should be based on clearly understood expectations for performance and growth.

George and Linda

With the foregoing discussion as background, let's look at the hypothetical situation of George and Linda. George is 65 and Linda is 3 years younger. They are newly retired, George having recently sold a successful business of which he was founder. They have three children who are doing well in their own careers, and who have given them five grandchildren, with prospects of more likely.

Their net worth is just over $100 million, consisting of two homes with equity of $6 million, George's retirement plan, which was rolled into an IRA, valued at $2,500,000, various brokerage accounts of around $50 million, invested in stocks and municipal bonds, two commercial properties, and two apartment complexes with equity of $37 million. The balance of their estate is cash, art, furnishings, automobiles, and a boat.

Several years ago they created a living trust at the urging of their attorney, who advised them of the benefits that it could provide, including the avoidance of probate, management of their affairs when they ultimately become incapable of doing so, estate tax savings, and their ability to distribute assets in accordance with their wishes. But with a $100 million net worth—even allowing for the benefit of their trust—their federal estate tax liability would be nearly $31 million, generally due in nine months following death. As they both enjoy good health and expect to live another 25 years, at a 3% annual growth rate, their estate could reach $209 million. Based upon current rates and exemptions, the resulting estate tax bill could be a whopping $75 million.

George's IRA will be hit even harder. On top of the federal estate tax liability, there will also be income taxes because IRAs do not receive a step up in income tax basis as do most other assets, which otherwise would alleviate gain as the assets pass from one generation to the next. The result is that less than 35 cents out of every hard-earned retirement plan dollar could ultimately get to his children.

With the help of their financial planner they've come to realize that estate planning is more than wills, trusts, and estate tax avoidance. The process starts with a discussion of their attitudes and beliefs and the legacy they desire to leave. Through this process they re-affirmed their desire to financially benefit their family as well as community, at death and during their lifetimes as well. And they concluded that a defining characteristic would be to transfer opportunities and incentives, not entitlements. With a new sense of purpose, they went to work to revise and enhance their plan.

But before George and Linda embark on any estate planning strategies, they should have a clear picture of not only their current, but future financial situation. Financial modeling, which shows details as to assets, cash flows, as well as both income and estate taxes, will allow them to not only more fully understand the issues and problems, but also the impact of the solutions. Above all, their first obligation must be to their own financial security. Any estate planning strategy that endangers that is not worth pursuing.

Advantage—Lifetime Transfers

George and Linda's situation is typical in that they have structured their affairs through the creation of their living trust, to transfer their assets at death. Unfortunately, this is *not* the way to obtain maximum advantage under the U.S. transfer tax laws, if their objective is to preserve wealth for the next generations, which they very much want to do.

The U.S. system of transfer taxation favors *lifetime* transfers rather than those taking place at death. First, there is a $15,000 (subject to inflation adjustment) annual gift tax exclusion, allowing both George and Linda to transfer $15,000 gift tax free to each of their children and grandchildren (or anyone else, for that matter), for a total of as much as $240,000 every year (3 children plus 5 grandchildren times $15,000 from both George and Linda). If they fail to use their annual exclusion in any year, they cannot make it up later. It is truly a "use it or lose it" proposition. Gifting $240,000 every year for 20 years would allow George and Linda to remove $4.8 million plus the projected growth on that of about $1.7 million (at 3%), for a total of $6.5 million from their estate. The penalty for George and Linda not doing this is the loss of over $2.6 million ($6.5 million × 40%) for their children and ultimately their grandchildren, in transfer taxes paid to Uncle Sam. And it's not just the lost tax money; it's what that tax money itself could have generated in income to the children and ultimately the grandchildren. Suitable for annual exclusion gifts are cash, marketable securities, and even interests in real estate or a family business.

It should be noted that certain payments made directly to educational institutions and for healthcare are not treated as taxable gifts requiring the use of the annual exclusion. For example, if George and Linda wished to pay for their grandchildren's tuition (grade school to graduate school), by writing a check directly to the institution, no gift would ensue. Payments directly to medical care providers, for health insurance premiums and certain other health care related expenses would likewise be exempt.

Another opportunity involves the making of a low interest rate loan. The loan should incorporate standard provisions for payment of principal and interest, collateral and maturity (though interest may accrue and the principal may "balloon" at maturity). And if the interest rate is at least equal to the "Applicable Federal Rate" (a rate based upon U.S. Treasury securities published monthly by the IRS) for the length of the note, typically much lower than for a comparable commercial note, no gift should result. If one of their children were to invest the proceeds of such a loan into a business or investment opportunity, they could potentially earn a return significantly greater than the loan interest.

By the way, this transaction can be done in reverse, with parents borrowing previously gifted funds from their children, or a trust on their behalf. By paying a high interest rate, they would be providing their children an attractive return while shifting wealth, gift tax free, to them.

Next, there is the opportunity to make use of their estate and gift tax exemption during their *lifetime* to remove the growth on those assets from their estate. Their exemptions are temporarily increased to $11.4 million each ($22.8 million per couple), adjusted for inflation, under the Tax Cuts and Jobs Act of 2017, through 2025. If not extended or repealed prior, the provision expires after 2025, at which point the exemption will return to $5.6 million, as adjusted for inflation. For example, a gift of $11.4 million growing at 3% would grow to $20.5 million in twenty years. Because the *growth* on $11.4 million is removed, a tax savings of $3.7 million could be achieved. As with the annual exclusion, suitable gifts include cash, marketable securities, real estate and family businesses. Generally speaking, assets with the greatest growth potential may warrant first consideration.

A gift in trust for children, continuing for the benefit of grandchildren and perhaps future generations, is considered a generation-skipping transaction. What's being skipped is the estate tax at each generation's death. Such a gift requires the allocation of the generation-skipping transfer tax (GST) exemption, which is equivalent to the current estate and gift tax exemption.

With intra-family transfers, valuation is all-important. The value of cash and publicly traded assets is readily determined. But so-called "hard to value" assets may require an appraisal wherein such factors as lack of marketability, lack of control and others are considered. Valuation adjustments (i.e., discounts) vary but 30–40% would not be unusual for a closely-held business or real estate partnership or limited liability company (LLC). Such discounts may have the effect of increasing wealth transfer opportunities. For example, George and Linda could make gifts of their commercial properties and apartments held in LLCs to their children or grandchildren (or, ideally, in a trust for their benefit). While acting as the managing member, they could retain control while taking advantage of a possible discount in the value of the gifted shares. They could use their $11.4 million exemptions for gifts of over $17.5 million in real estate LLC interests, assuming a 35% valuation discount applied. A similar discount may be available upon their death.

It should be noted that the IRS has sought to include previously gifted assets (e.g., closely held business interests) in the transferor's estate where control of the asset by the transferor was retained. So careful planning involving qualified tax counsel is important here.

As we explore the various strategies which follow, I hasten to point out that it is important to consider the implications that asset transfers may have on property tax assessment as well as loan covenants on real estate and other assets.

A Matter of Trust

A question often arises of what is the best way to make the gifts: outright or in trust. Outright gifts are the simplest. But they have the disadvantage of exposing the gifts to the beneficiary's creditors, judgments, divorce, and possible mismanagement. Further, the goal of wealth transfers should not be to merely move assets down a generation, but rather to *remove* them from the transfer tax system, protecting them from being taxed in the estates of future generations. These outcomes, asset protection, third party management and estate tax relief, can only be achieved through the use of an irrevocable trust. Thus, trusts can hold assets that are gifted during lifetime as well as those transferred at death. Often the trusts are combined at the parent's death for simplicity of administration.

Many states have modified their Rule Against Perpetuities laws which, generally, limits a trust's duration to the death of the last surviving beneficiary alive at the trust's creation, or when the trust becomes irrevocable, plus 21 years. Trusts in some states may now continue for 500 years or more, providing family wealth protection for many generations. Often this type of trust is referred to as a Dynasty Trust.

Trustee duties can reside exclusively with a trust company, providing institutional independence and expertise. Alternatively, trust beneficiaries may serve as trustees, potentially elected by other beneficiaries for a specified term of years, or the beneficiaries may serve as co-trustee alongside the independent trustee, supporting the success of a multi-generation trust. Various Trust Advisors can be named to guide the trustee(s) on matters involving trust distribution, investment, and business management. Other features to be considered include a Trust Protector whose functions may include safeguarding the original intent of the trust, including altering trust language, changing trust situs, and replacing trustees. Another trust feature includes the authority of the trustee to decant the trust—modify the existing trust by "pouring" the assets of the trust into another to eliminate unwanted provisions in the existing trust, or add desired benefits in a new trust.

A trust may be drafted to allow George and Linda to pay the trust's income tax while they are alive. This is often referred to as an intentionally defective grantor trust (IDGT). The "defect" is that the trust is ignored for income tax purposes. Thus, the income, losses, deductions and gains pass through to the grantor. Though accelerating the growth of trust assets while shifting wealth, a peculiarity in the tax code does not consider this a gift (a feature allowing this provision to be "switched off" can also be incorporated).

IDGTs, GRATs and QPRTs

If George and Linda were desirous of transferring assets in excess of the annual exclusion and estate and gift exemption, without incurring a gift tax, they could sell an asset to a trust. As normally structured, the trust will make a down payment with the balance in a note bearing interest at the Applicable Federal Rate. Notes may be interest only and have a balloon feature. In order to avoid gain recognition or "recapture" of negative capital accounts, the sale must be to a trust that is defective for income tax purposes. As previously mentioned, this means that George and Linda as the grantors would be responsible for the tax liability on trust income, although the note transaction itself (i.e. principal and interest) would be non-taxable. Because the trust sale would not be recognized for income tax purposes, as with a gift, the tax basis in the asset carries over to the trust.

A general rule of thumb is that the trust must have assets (typically transferred by prior gift) of at least 10% of the value of the assets sold to it (and purchased by the trust). As in the prior example, assuming a 35% valuation discount would apply to an initial gift of $17.5 million, the gift would be valued at $11.4 million, which would be offset by the exemption. George and Linda could then sell additional assets to the trust, if they desired. This strategy has the effect of shifting the return (i.e., growth and income), in excess of the Applicable Federal Rate, to the trust (Table 2.1).

A Self-Cancelling Installment Note (SCIN) is an alternative to a traditional installment note. By its terms, a SCIN is cancelled at the seller's (i.e., note maker's) death. This removes the remaining note balance from the seller's estate, saving the estate tax otherwise due on the value of the note. In consideration for the forgiveness feature, the note must carry a "risk premium": a higher face amount or higher interest rate. Yet another alternative is a private annuity, which like the SCIN, is also extinguished at death, but with no required risk premium. The catch is that payments must continue for the seller's life, even if in excess of the original note value. Both the SCIN

Table 2.1 Sale to Intentionally Defective Grantor Trust (IDGT)

Let's take a look at an example:	
$10 million 10 year note sale	
Assumed property return	6.0%
Applicable Federal Rate (note rate)	2.9%
Trust retained return	3.1%
Future value of trust retained wealth in 10 years (net of note and interest)	$4,599,222

and the Private Annuity can be useful if the seller expects shorter than normal life expectancy, for example due to impaired health, as less than the note value (sale price less down payment) is likely to be included in the estate. The pros and cons of each relative to a traditional installment note (including treatment of gain recognition, interest deductibility, collateralization, among other factors) must be carefully considered.

One potential disadvantage of the IDGT strategy is that while no gain is recognized upon asset sale to the trust, the customary basis step-up at death is foregone. Since the trust ceases to be "defective" for income tax purposes upon the grantor's death, a subsequent sale of the asset by the trust will trigger recognition of any gains, with an ensuing tax liability. A remedy may be for the transferor to buy the asset back for cash (extinguishing an installment note if still outstanding), returning the asset to the transferor's estate for basis step-up upon death.

Another way to leverage their exemptions would be through the use of a Grantor Retained Annuity Trust or GRAT. This technique entails George and Linda each creating a trust for a period of years, say ten years, into which they would transfer an asset, perhaps LLC units in one of their properties. George and Linda could serve as trustee. During the trust term, they would receive income from the trust and continue to make investment decisions as they otherwise would. Upon trust termination in ten years, trust assets plus appreciation thereon, will pass to the children without tax. The advantage of this strategy from a transfer planning standpoint is the value of the gift to their children is the present value of the income interest using "120% of the Applicable Federal Midterm Rate." As it is likely their real estate would outperform this rate by a substantial margin, a significant amount of future appreciation can be shifted. The result is a substantial leveraging of George and Linda's exemptions. The downside, if the asset underperforms, is that they would have accomplished less or perhaps no wealth transfer, with the value of the asset still in their estate and having used a portion or all of their gift tax exemption (Fig. 2.2 and Table 2.2).

There is a catch. The GRAT requires that George and Linda, as grantors of the trust, actually survive the trust term. Should they die prior to the ten years that we have used in our example, a portion of the asset will be included in their estate.

In a similar strategy, George and Linda could each create a Qualified Personal Residence Trust or QPRT for a term of years and transfer one of their homes into it. Again, George and Linda could serve as trustee. They would continue to live in the home and would receive the continued enjoyment of its use, as well as the responsibility for the upkeep, taxes, insurance, etc.

George and Linda create trust and transfer property

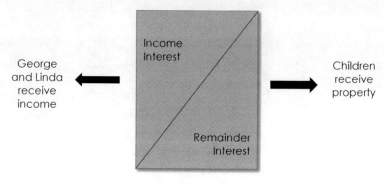

Fig. 2.2 Grantor Retained Annuity Trust (GRAT)

Table 2.2 GRAT example

Let's take a look at the following example:	
10 year GRAT	
10% payout (i.e. 6.5% yield on property discounted at 35%)	
Property value	$10,000,000
Less 35% discount	$3,500,000
Gift net of discount	$6,500,000
120% of Applicable Federal Midterm Rate	3.2%
Present value of remainder interest (taxable gift)	$931,398
Estimated property value in 10 years at 3% growth	$13,439,000

Upon termination of the trust, the home would pass to their children. The obvious question of where George and Linda would live is addressed by their arranging a lease, at a fair market rate, after the trust term allowing them to occupy the residence for as long as they chose. Again, the benefit of this arrangement is that it allows George and Linda to dramatically discount the transfer of the home to the children for gift tax purposes. Additionally, lease payments made by the parents would not be considered gifts, thereby providing the opportunity for additional transfers to the children (Table 2.3).

In addition to having to survive the term of the trust, another drawback shared by both the GRAT and QPRT strategies is that they generally allow you only to move the asset down one generation, rather than to remove it from the transfer tax system. This results from the inability to allocate the GST exemption when the gift is made. However, viewed in the context of a comprehensive estate plan, these strategies may still be useful.

Table 2.3 Qualified Personal Residence Trust (QPRT) example

As an example:	
10 year QPRT	
Property value (excludes mortgage)	$3,500,000
120% of Applicable Federal Midterm Rate	3.2%
Present value of remainder interest (taxable gift)	$2,005,570
Estimated property value in 10 years at 3% growth	$4,704,000

The Freeze

An effective strategy to put a lid on the value of the estate, shifting future appreciation to future generations, is the use of a preferred LLC or partnership freeze. This strategy would involve the creation of a new LLC to which George and Linda would contribute assets such as their real estate. The new LLC would consist of a frozen preferred interest (comparable to non-voting preferred stock), a managing member growth interest (comparable to voting common stock) and a non-managing member growth interest (comparable to non-voting common stock).

They would transfer by gift, utilizing their exemptions, the non-managing member growth interest to the irrevocable trust. They would retain the preferred interest and the managing member growth interest. The preferred interest would receive a "qualified payment" comparable to a cumulative preferred stock fixed rate dividend payable on a regular basis. The value of the preferred interest is determined by appraisal, considering the fixed cumulative preferred return (e.g., 8%). The growth interest must have a value of at least 10% of the value of the whole (Table 2.4).

Because the preferred interest bears a fixed cumulative payment, its value is fixed, freezing its value in the estate. Any appreciation in property values and cash distributions in excess of that required to make the payment on the preferred interest could inure to the growth interest.

Table 2.4 Typical structure of partnership freeze

Share type	%	Ownership
Non-managing member preferred (frozen)	90	Family trust
Non-managing member growth	9	Irrevocable trust for children and grandchildren
Managing member growth	1	Family trust

Advantages of this strategy include the following:

* Retained control through the managing member interest
* Retention of income through the preferred interest
* Preferred payment flexibility, including:
  - Payments in kind
  - Delay for up to four years from due date (provided that interest is charged)
* Basis step up at death on the retained preferred and managing member interests

A Taxing History

As we've discussed, there are a number of transfer taxes in place in our country today. They apply to both U.S. citizens and residents. In 1916 Congress created the estate tax which is levied on the transfer of property by the estate owner at death. Also, many states impose their own transfer tax.

The federal estate tax rates are progressive and range from 18 to 40%. Recognizing that individuals with sizable estates could give most of their property away prior to death in an attempt to avoid an estate tax, in 1932 Congress created the gift tax. It applies to all non-charitable transfers during one's lifetime. The gift tax rates were unified in 1976 and now are the same as the estate tax. This should dispel the notion that you can just "give it all away before death" (Table 2.5).

Another element of transfer taxation is the GSTT. Wealthy individuals were leaving their estates in trusts providing income for their heirs, but which escaped estate taxes as they passed from generation to generation. But in 1976, Congress enacted the GSTT. Retroactively repealed and replaced in 1986, the GSTT generally imposes a tax, in addition to the gift and estate tax, for transfers to individuals two or more generations below the transferor (i.e., grandchildren). The rate (assessed at the highest estate tax rate) and exemption is the same as that for the gift and estate tax. So an individual may make a gift to grandchildren or more remote generations of up to $5.6 million ($11.4 million, adjusted for inflation, through 2025). An exception to the GST Tax may apply for gifts to a grandchild or a trust for his or her benefit, which qualifies for the annual exclusion.

Table 2.5   Federal gift and estate tax

Taxable gift or estate		Tentative tax	
From	To	Tax	Rate on excess (%)
$0	$10,000	$0	18
10,000	20,000	1800	20
20,000	40,000	3800	22
40,000	60,000	8200	24
60,000	80,000	13,000	26
80,000	100,000	18,200	28
100,000	150,000	23,800	30
150,000	250,000	38,800	32
250,000	500,000	70,800	34
500,000	750,000	155,800	37
750,000	1,000,000	248,300	39
1,000,000	And above	345,800	40

Gift and estate exempt amount/credit[a]	
Credit	Exempt amount
$1,945,800	$5,000,000

[a]Subject to inflation adjustment. The Tax Cuts and Jobs Act of 2017 nearly doubled the 2018 inflation adjusted exemption amount to $11.18 million ($22.36 million per married couple), effective for years 2018–2025. Unless extended, the exemption reverts to inflation-adjusted amount per prior law

So the question arises of how to pay the estate tax which will be unavoidable, considering the various planning strategies that have or will be implemented, and which were presented in this chapter and in Chapter 3, Charitable Planning, and Chapter 4, Business Succession, which follow.

Essentially, there are four options, as summarized below (Table 2.6).

The economics of life insurance varies with gender, age, and condition of health and whether one or two lives are being insured. For George and Linda, who both enjoy reasonably good health, life insurance may represent the best solution. They can acquire a $20 million policy for about 32¢ on the dollar.

So as to exclude the policy from their taxable estates, it can be owned by an irrevocable trust they have created as part of their estate planning process. The premiums may be structured as gifts, loans, or paid from income from property transferred to the trust. Upon their death, the tax-free insurance proceeds can be used to purchase assets from George and Linda's estate, providing cash for estate tax payment.

Life insurance will be discussed in greater detail in Chapter 6.

Table 2.6 Four ways to pay

Source (assumption)	Cost for each dollar of tax	Implications
Cash	$1.00	– Requires time to accumulate – Opportunity cost of holding – Consumes working capital/liquid reserves
Sell assets (at 80¢ on the dollar)	$1.25	– Future market conditions unknown – Sale must close in 9 months, FET due date prompting "estate sale" discount
Borrow from a bank (10 year/7% interest loan, 35% bracket)	$1.26	– Financing may be unavailable or unattractive – Encumbers property, increasing risk – Reduces cash flow
Life insurance (husband and wife age 65, standard rate, non smoker, at life expectancy)	32¢	– Requires insurability – Opportunity cost of premiums

Thinking About the Unthinkable

Estate planning entails more than planning your own estate. It should involve planning for the estates of your children as well. While the thought of the incapacity or death of a child is nearly unthinkable, proper planning requires that we do just that. Adult children should, at a minimum, have a will, power of attorney and a health care directive. The latter will ensure that should they become incapable of making their own health care decisions, that the parent, another family member, or their spouse could do so. As their estate grows, they should create their own trust which, among other things, may be helpful in preserving the separate property identity of assets you have gifted to them. Of course, a pre-marital agreement may further protect their assets in the unfortunate—but all too likely event—that their marriage ends in divorce.

Postscript—Keys to a Family Flourishing

In their book Complete Family Wealth, the authors express that they have been privileged to work with and to research families—worldwide, which have flourished over multiple generations. Their research, in particular, has focused on families who have successfully transitioned a significant family enterprise through at least two generations, who "measure their achievements in decades, even centuries." From this, they have distilled the following key elements in family flourishing[4]:

- At some point in their early history, flourishing families form the intention to build not only a great fortune but also a great family. This is the fundamental intention, without which little else can follow.
- These families articulate and share their core values, and they keep those values alive through example, education, and further discussions.
- These families respect and encourage individual differences. They support members' separation and development of individual identities as members of the family discover their own dreams.
- These families keep their collective focus on their strengths. They face challenges squarely but don't let liabilities become their focus.
- Flourishing families share history with family stories that are told and retold through the generations. They sustain and celebrate their traditions and rituals.
- Parents see themselves as both teachers and learners.
- Such families understand the importance of individual stages of development and integrate that understanding into parenting.

A carefully crafted estate plan will embrace and help sustain these factors in the years and generations to come.

Questions to Consider

- Does your estate plan provide for the distribution of your wealth in a fashion consistent with your vision for your legacy for family and society?

---

[4]James E. Hughes, Jr., Susan E. Massenzio, and Keith Whitaker, *Complete Family Wealth* (Hoboken, NJ: Wiley, 2018).

- Have you discussed your plan with your heirs, eliciting their input and preparing them to be effective stewards of your wealth?
- Does your plan contribute to the typical pattern of "shirtsleeves to shirtsleeves in three generations"?
- Do your current arrangements merely move your assets to the next generation or instead remove them from the transfer tax system?
- How big is your estate tax now and in the future and what impact will that have on your plan for wealth transfer and retention?

3

Charitable Planning

For it is in giving that we receive.
—Saint Francis of Assisi, Italian Catholic Friar, deacon, and preacher

For those with more than enough wealth the question becomes what to do with the surplus. Realistically, everyone dying with a taxable estate is a philanthropist—their causes are the federal and state governments, exacted by federal estate and potentially, state inheritance or estate taxes. For those wishing to exert some control over what has been referred to as "involuntary philanthropy" they may be able to reduce their estate tax obligation by employing some of the strategies discussed in Chapter 2. This chapter addresses methods to accomplish "voluntary philanthropy", directing assets to your desired causes both during your lifetime and at death while reaping both income and estate tax benefits. Such activities can also be a means of uniting family members in a common cause and even elevating the visibility of the family and its members. Let's discuss each.

In order to appreciate the income, gift, and estate tax benefits, it should be helpful to consider the range of various forms in which charitable gifts can be made. Gifts can be of cash, or property such as bonds, stocks, real estate and artwork. They can also be structured as what I call "no strings attached" and "strings attached" gifts. The former is basically outright gifts to charity. The latter consists of qualified arrangements wherein you retain the income from the asset for a period of time with the charity receiving the asset afterwards. Alternatively, the charity may be given the income first with, typically, your children receiving the asset afterwards. Finally, charitable gifts can be made during lifetime and at death. The timing will

© The Author(s) 2019
R. P. Rojeck, *Wealth*,
https://doi.org/10.1007/978-3-030-24497-2_3

determine the nature and magnitude of the income, gift, and estate tax benefits.

For income tax purposes, rules governing charitable contributions address both valuation and deduction limits. Cash is, of course, deductible at its value. For gifts to public charities, appreciated assets are valued based upon their fair market value if a cash sale of the property would have been long term capital gain. Cash contributions are deductible up to 60% of adjusted gross income (through 2025 under Tax Cuts and Jobs Act of 2017, then 50%), or 30% if appreciated property. Unused deductions are eligible for a five-year carry forward. Different rules apply to gifts to a private foundation, which we shall discuss shortly. For gift and estate tax purposes, gifts are valued at fair market value with no deduction limit.

Incidentally, it is generally advisable to satisfy a charitable gift with an appreciated asset rather than cash. This is so because as a tax exempt entity, a charity will pay no capital gains tax upon sale of the appreciated share of stock or parcel of real estate you may have gifted it. Hence, the full value of the asset is available for the charity's use and the donor is relieved of the capital gains tax she may otherwise have ultimately paid on the appreciated asset.

You should also be aware that not all assets are suitable for charitable giving. For example, a charity may refuse a gift of contaminated land to which a liability for clean up could attach. They may not be willing to accept a fractional interest in an entity such as an LLC owning real estate, which may be unmarketable. By law, a charitable remainder trust will lose its tax exemption if funded with debt-encumbered real estate. And a private foundation is restricted in its ability to hold a closely-held business interest. These restrictions, and others notwithstanding, creative planning can still yield significant benefits from charitable giving strategies.

CRATs, CRUTs, CLATs, and CLUTs

With that as background let's take a look at some examples, starting with one of the most common arrangements, the charitable remainder trust. In the most common version of this arrangement you create and fund a charitable trust that distributes income to you, and perhaps your spouse, for your lifetime. Upon your death the trust terminates and the assets pass to the specified charity. The income can be expressed as a dollar amount (a Charitable Remainder Annuity Trust or CRAT) or a percentage (a Charitable Remainder Uni-Trust or CRUT). CRUTs come in various forms as well.

Charitable Remainder Trusts are useful when the donor is desirous of disposing of a highly appreciated asset (for example, stock or real estate) but is concerned about the resulting capital gains tax which could exceed 35% (federal capital gains tax, Affordable Care Tax and state income tax). Because a CRT is tax exempt, the asset can be sold and the entire proceeds reinvested. Income distributed is taxed under a four-tier arrangement in the following order: ordinary income, capital gain, other income (e.g., tax free income) and finally distribution of corpus (i.e., basis). The trust can continue for a period of up to 20 years or for the lifetime of the donor(s) or other beneficiary (e.g., children).

The advantages of a CRT include the following:

- Upfront income tax deduction based on the present value of the charity's remainder interest
- Deferral of gain recognition on sale of the contributed asset
- Estate tax deduction
- Potential creditor protection of trust assets
- Benefiting a charitable cause, including you own private foundation (Fig. 3.1 and Table 3.1).

A strategy achieving similar results deserves mention here. A charitable gift annuity works in a similar fashion with the primary distinction of saving you the time and the expense of creating the charitable trust. The sponsoring charity pays the donor a specified percentage of the value of the gift. The American Council on Gift Annuities (www.acga-web.org) publishes rate charts with suggested payout rates for these arrangements, which considers such factors as investment return assumptions and mortality rates.

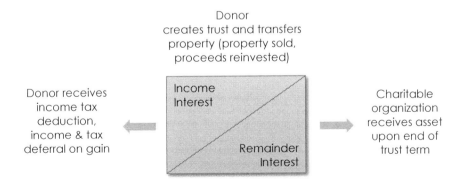

Fig. 3.1 Charitable Remainder Trust (CRT)

Table 3.1 Charitable Remainder Annuity Trust (CRAT) example

Let's turn to an example of a Charitable Remainder Annuity Trust providing a lifetime income for an individual age 65:	
Property Value	$10,000,000
Income %	5%
Annual Annuity	$500,000
120% of Applicable Federal Midterm Rate	3.2%
Present Value of Donor's Annuity	$6,441,645
Present Value of Charitable Remainder/Donor's Income Tax Deduction	$3,585,197
Income Tax Savings (@ 40%)	$1,434,079

One might say that a Charitable Lead Trust is the mirror image of a CRT, in that the identities of the income and remainder beneficiaries are reversed with the charity receiving the income up-front. Further, the asset most often passes to the donor's children rather than to the donor. The result is that it is an effective way to benefit charity as well as transfer wealth to the next generation.

While a CRT is income tax exempt, that is not the case for a CLT, but the trust will receive a deduction for income paid to the charitable income beneficiary. There is an exception to this rule: if a trust is structured as a defective trust, its income is reportable by the donor, not the trust, and the donor will receive an income tax deduction in the first year equal to the present value of the charitable distributions (i.e., the income tax deduction is front loaded). The trade-off is that in the following years, the donor must include trust income in his own income without the benefit of charitable deductions or income from the trust.

If you remember the GRAT described in Chapter 2, the CLAT produces virtually an identical transfer tax result. Unfortunately, a CLAT suffers from the same restriction in not being a good multi-generation transfer strategy (i.e., the GST exemption cannot be allocated at trust inception when the gift is deemed made). But it can be an effective tool in moving assets down one generation. In evaluating this strategy one must consider the period of time the beneficiary must wait until the termination of the charity's income interest and the beneficiary's age at that time. Unlike a CRT, the duration of a CLT is not limited to a specified number of years.

The advantages of a CLAT arrangement include the following:

• Ability to lower the deemed value of a gift to your children, thereby leveraging your estate and gift tax exemption

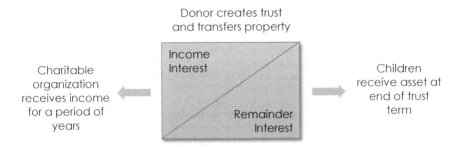

Fig. 3.2 Charitable Lead Trust (CLT)

- Removing the asset, plus all the growth, from your estate
- Potential creditor protection of CLAT assets
- Benefiting a charitable cause (Fig. 3.2).

Often referred to as a Testamentary CLAT or TCLAT, Charitable Lead Trusts can be created at death under the family trust and provide for payments to charity for a period of years, with the family receiving the asset afterwards. The estate is entitled to an estate tax charitable deduction equal to the present value of the charity's income interest. One version of this strategy is to provide that the number of years be determined with reference to an ensuing charitable deduction to result in a zero estate tax liability in the deceased trustor's estate. This is often referred to as a "zero estate tax plan."

Private Foundation

Yet another consideration is a Private Foundation structured as either a tax-exempt trust or corporation under section 501(c) of the Internal Revenue Code. A Private Foundation creates a family-controlled entity through which charitable activities can take place, often institutionalizing a family name in the community for philanthropic activities. While gifts to a Private Foundation generate an income tax deduction, limits are lower than those to a public charity. For example, cash gifts are subject to a deduction limitation of 30% of AGI versus 60% for a public charity. Gifts of appreciated property qualify for a 20% deduction versus 30% if to a public charity. Also, except for publicly traded stock held for more than 12 months, gifts of appreciated assets generally require the donor to use the tax basis rather than market value.

Private Foundations are subject to numerous rules and restrictions. Following are just a few:

- An excise tax of 2% is imposed on the foundation's net investment income.
- Must distribute a minimum amount equal to 5% of investment assets annually. (Incidentally, these two restrictions generally also apply to Charitable Lead Trusts.)
- Self-dealing restrictions prohibit the following transactions with disqualified persons:

  - Sale, exchange, or leasing of property
  - Lending of money or any other extension of credit, other than interest free loans from the donor to the foundation
  - Furnishing of goods, services, or facilities other than from the donor to the foundation without charge
  - Payment of compensation by the foundation to the donor unless such amounts are reasonable and necessary to carrying on the foundation's exempt purposes and are not excessive
  - Transfer of any income or assets from the foundation to the donor or for the donor's use or benefit
  - Certain transfers of mortgaged property to the foundation.

- Disqualified persons consist of:

  - A substantial contributor to the foundation (defined as $5000 or more; if more than 2% of total annual contributions)
  - A foundation manager
  - An owner of more than 20% of an entity that is a substantial contributor to the foundation
  - A member of the family of any person named in the three
  - categories above
  - Another private foundation controlled by the same person.

- The following restrictions apply with respect to ownership of a closely-held business:

  - Cannot hold more than 20% of an entity's voting interests, less the percentage owned by all disqualified persons
  - May hold non-voting interest, but only if all disqualified persons together hold less than 20% of voting interests

– A 5-year grace period exists for disposal of excess holdings, if received as a result of a gift or bequest.

A Private Foundation may be the recipient of the remainder interest of a charitable remainder trust. However, the income tax deduction will be governed by the lower private foundation limits. A Private Foundation is generally not, however, a suitable recipient of the income interest of a charitable lead trust, as it may cause estate inclusion of an otherwise estate tax excludable asset.

In a similar way that a charitable gift annuity is a simpler and lower cost option to a charitable remainder trust, a donor advised fund may likewise offer greater simplicity and lower cost than a private foundation. Often sponsored by community foundations, donor advised funds eliminate the need to create a trust or corporation as the legal structure is already in place. You are permitted the higher income tax deductions associated with the public charity. The donor advised fund will also do the record keeping, assist in identifying suitable grant candidates, do the tax reporting, and even manage your funds, if you wish. Finally, most funds allow the family name to be identified with it, if that is your desire.

Advantage-Lifetime Transfers (Again)

Just as in wealth transfer planning for family members, the U.S. tax system favors lifetime charitable giving over charitable bequests at death. Since there is no distinction in the estate tax benefit—one's estate is reduced either way, the advantage is owing to the income tax deduction derived from lifetime gifts. For example, assume an individual gifts $500,000 annually to her Private Foundation. In an assumed 40% tax bracket (federal and state combined), that gives rise to a $200,000 annual tax savings. Assuming this continues for 20 years and the tax savings is reinvested at 5% net, the additional accumulation is $6,613,000. This could be used to enhance either a transfer to the family or the foundation. And actually there is another income tax advantage: income earned by the foundation is subject to a modest 2% federal income tax rate, compared to her 40% combined personal rate.

In fact, as illustrated in the following Wealth Management Plan, you can see how incorporating multiple structures within a comprehensive financial plan may enhance wealth accumulation and transfer (Fig. 3.3).

	Revocable Trust	Irrevocable Trust	Private Foundation
Control[a]	Family	Family	Family
Income Tax[b]	Taxable	Taxable	Exempt
Estate Tax[c]	Taxable	Exempt	Exempt
Creditors[d]	Exposed	Protected	Protected

[a]Family members can serve as trustees or officers or retain discretion to appoint and remove third parties
[b]Trusts can mitigate income tax through investment decisions (e.g. municipal bonds). Irrevocable trust, if "defective" while grantor alive, is untaxed, as trustor pays tax on trust income. If non-grantor trust, may be situated in state with no income tax
[c]Irrevocable Trust, if situated in a state allowing perpetual trusts, may escape estate taxation for multiple generations
[d]Irrevocable trusts generally afford protection from creditors of beneficiaries

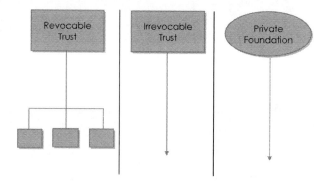

Fig. 3.3   Wealth Management Plan

Other Strategies

Seldom discussed yet a potentially valuable charitable vehicle is a Supporting Organization. As the name suggests, its purpose is to make grants to other publicly supported entities.

In contrast to a Private Foundation, a Supporting Organization carries public charity status, hence gifts enjoy more favorable tax treatment (e.g., 60% versus 30% AGI limit for cash gifts, 30% versus 20% AGI limit for appreciated property, etc.). Further, they are exempt from Private Foundation excise tax and administrative requirements, resulting in greater suitability for gifts of appreciated assets such as real estate or a closely held business.

The trade-off is that, generally, a majority of the governing board of the Supporting Organization must be appointed by the publicly supported charity or charities, placing the donor and or his family in a minority position. But given the supported organization's desire to foster such arrangements, they strive to be good philanthropic partners with the donor and the causes he or she favors.

A common use for a Supporting Organization is in conjunction with a Community Foundation. The foundation, which appoints a majority of the Supporting Organization's board, can provide administrative support (e.g., investment management, bookkeeping, tax filings, meeting facilities, grant administration) yet need not necessarily be the sole beneficiary of the Supporting Organization's grants.

Another strategy is a Retained Life Estate with Gift Annuity of a primary or secondary residence or farm. For individuals in their mid-60 s or older, this can be a great strategy to turn their home into a source of income, as well as a means of philanthropy. You enter an arrangement with a charity to receive monthly payments for a period up to your lifetime while continuing to live in your home or on your farm. This generates a current income tax deduction equal to the present value of the charity's remainder interest (home value less present value of projected payments to be received by you). You remain responsible for any mortgage payments, property tax, and upkeep. Upon your death, the property passes to the charity free of estate tax. If you do not need the income, you will receive a larger current income tax deduction (Table 3.2).

Another strategy is a Conservation Easement. Property consisting of farm, timber, pasture, or wetlands may hold potential for conservation purposes for plant and animal habitat, water conservation or simply as open space. The owner can confer an easement on his property, to a qualified entity, restricting future development or activities in the interest of protecting such attributes. The recipient is typically a not-for-profit land trust. Such easements follow the land, whether it is retained or ultimately sold. The owner retains all other rights, such as occupancy and agricultural, farming, or ranching activities. Such an easement does not necessarily grant public access.

Table 3.2 Retained Life Estate with Gift Annuity example

As an example for a couple age 65:	
Property Value (excludes mortgage[a])	$5,000,000
Life annuity received annually	$78,000
Present Value of Charitable Remainder	$546,092
Donor's Income Tax Deduction	
Annual annuity income as well as the charitable deduction will be higher at older ages or in the case of a single individual	

[a]Relatively few charities holding a license to issue charitable gift annuities are willing to issue a life annuity when a personal residence is encumbered by a mortgage. Those licensed charities which do so typically subtract the monthly mortgage payments from the periodic annuity payment made to the donor

The value of the easement is based on the reduction of the value from its highest and best use (e.g., for commercial development) to its status subject to the easement. This reduction gives rise to a current income tax deduction, possibly property tax relief, and value reduction for gift and estate tax purposes.

A simple strategy if you have a traditional IRA (e.g., a rollover from a profit-sharing or pension plan) and have attained age 70½ is to make your charitable contributions from it. You can contribute up to $100,000 annually, while excluding the $100,000 distribution from your income and counting it toward your minimum required distribution. This provision is sometimes referred to as a charitable IRA rollover. Charitable gifts must be made directly to a charity by the IRA custodian, and a private foundation, supporting organizations or donor advised fund (and certain other charitable vehicles) is not a qualifying recipient for the purpose of this rule. This provision may be particularly helpful if your charitable contributions will exceed the AGI limit for the year. A traditional IRA (and most retirement plans in general) may also be a wise choice for a charitable bequest at death. Since retirement assets generally do not receive a basis step up at death, the deferred income will be taxable to your child or grandchild when distributed. Not so for a charity; it will receive the funds income tax free.

Final Thoughts

As a high net worth individual, you and your charitable entity will be called upon and perhaps already have, for contributions to any number of worthy causes, often with offers of a seat at the board of directors for the organization. Assuming your resources, time, and money aren't unlimited, I offer the following thoughts on how such opportunities should be considered. They are drawn from the practical experience of longtime San Diego community leader and philanthropist Malin Burnham.[1]

* Focus your charitable donations of cash, property, and volunteer time on those mostly aligned with your family's values. If you have established a charitable foundation, its mission and purpose should be clear, and grant-making activities appropriately aligned.

[1]Malin Burnham and Michael S. Malone, *Community Before Self: Seventy Years of Making Waves* (Charleston, SC: Advantage Media Group, 2016).

- Establish a budget for annual gifts, knowing that the occasional larger gift opportunity will come along from time to time. Private foundations are required to distribute 5% of their assets (after expenses) annually, which also should coincide with a sustainable spending rate using an endowment approach.
- It's often difficult to determine if a number of small gifts are making a difference to the organizations receiving them. And a small gift usually results in a weak voice in communicating your preferences, ideas and expectations.
- Consider making the gift to a specific project you feel is important, rather than to the organization itself.
- Favor projects where your gift can have the greatest leverage. Will your gift be a catalyst to attract gifts from others? Is the program or activity scalable and sustainable on an ongoing basis or will it require ongoing funding?
- Charities are businesses too. Favor organizations run like a business with good leadership, a track record of results, and efficient operations.
- Don't demand a board position, but expect accountability and periodic progress reports for the project.

Finally, if you already have or are contemplating a private foundation, consider using a firm to which you can outsource such tasks as writing a mission statement, preparing financials, administering grants, completing annual tax filings, etc. Consultants are also available to help you identify charitable causes and to structure your gifts in such a way as to achieve maximum impact from your charitable dollars.

Returning to George and Linda, after giving the subject of philanthropy a good deal of thought, including discussions with their three children and consultation with their financial planner, they have decided to create a family foundation and seed it with $5 million of appreciated securities, 5% of their current estate. Given the 5% private foundation distribution requirement, this establishes an annual giving budget of $250,000. They have also provided that an additional 25% of their estate will pass to the foundation upon the death of the survivor, including George's IRA which, in addition to estate tax, would also have been subject to income tax as distributed. Their children will serve on the foundation's grants and investment committees. They are proud of the foundation's simply-stated mission, which reads: "Benefiting our community through support of children's education and healthcare."

Questions to Consider

- Have you considered how much wealth is "enough" for your family and how your wealth could be directed to benefit your community and society as well?
- Are you employing strategies to take maximum advantage of income and estate tax benefits of charitable giving?
- Have you involved your family in your philanthropic activities? Are you preparing them to be effective stewards of your philanthropic legacy?
- Is your giving focused and designed to achieve maximum impact for the causes you support?

4

Business Succession

It's been said "Entrepreneurship is living a few years of your life like most people won't so you can spend the rest of your life like most people can't". Risk-taking and acceptance of delayed gratification are hallmarks of the entrepreneurial mentality. Often, a closely-held business constitutes the lion's share of the owner's estate and planning for its continuation or ultimate disposition can take on significance even beyond its proportion of family wealth. After all, it is the manifestation of years, possibly generations of the inspiration, hard work, sacrifice, risk-taking, and even identity of the founder and perhaps family members following in his or her footsteps.

In planning for business succession and disposition, I normally see four scenarios:

Scenario One: Shared ownership with non-family members with the goal of ultimately selling the business to this other person upon retirement, disability, or death.
Scenario Two: Family involvement with the goal to sustain family ownership.
Scenario Three: Sole or substantial ownership with a goal to sell to several executives or employees.
Scenario Four: Sale to a yet to be identified third party, such as a private investor or group or potential public offering as the exit strategy.

Let's discuss each, in turn, starting with Scenario One.

© The Author(s) 2019
R. P. Rojeck, *Wealth*,
https://doi.org/10.1007/978-3-030-24497-2_4

Sale to a Co-owner

As closely held businesses have no ready market, the goal for planning purposes is to create a market by contract. This is referred to as a buy and sell agreement. It can minimize potential disputes and resulting business disruption should any one of a number of scenarios unfold. This is one of the most basic business documents, yet one often absent or poorly drafted. Certain triggering events are self-evident: retirement, disability, and death. Yet there are many other events that should be addressed, including divorce, personal bankruptcy, voluntary and involuntary termination of employment, transfer to family and non-family members, and—if a professional firm—loss of professional license.

And then there is the matter of who is doing the buying and the selling. Is it the entity, known as an "entity purchase" agreement, or specifically a stock redemption in the case of a corporation? Or is it the owners themselves, known as a "cross-purchase" agreement?

In the following example, shareholder A's stock is being purchased due to a triggering event. The basic problem with an entity purchase is that while shareholder B's ownership increases from 50 to 100%, he generally doesn't receive an increase in the basis of his ownership interest because it was the entity that purchased shareholder A's shares. This problem is remedied in a cross-purchase agreement as B's basis is increased by the purchase price he pays. A cross-purchase structure, however, is not without its limitations as well, including added complexity in multiple shareholder scenarios, especially when life insurance policies are used to help fund the agreement.

Still another consideration is the tax bracket of the entity, if a C corporation is involved, compared with that of the individual shareholders. The lower the corporation's tax bracket, the lower the after-tax cost of the purchase price as more dollars are available to make the purchase which is an after-tax event. So the structure of the firm as a "C" or "S" corporation, limited liability company, or partnership, will bear on the decision.

Combining features of both an entity purchase and a cross-purchase results in what is commonly referred to as a "wait and see" or hybrid arrangement which may produce an optimum result in tax efficiency and flexibility. A hybrid agreement typically provides that the entity will have a right of first refusal. If the entity declines to purchase the business interest, the individual owners may do so. Life insurance policies funding the agreement may either be owned individually, in a trust, or partnership, depending on the nature of the entity as a C corporation or S corporation, LLC or partnership (Fig. 4.1).

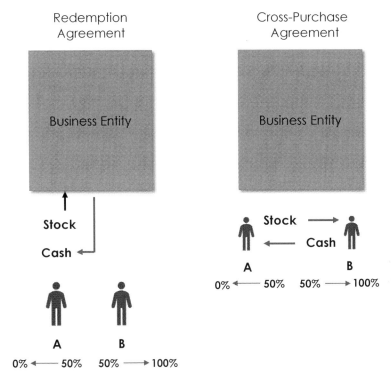

Fig. 4.1 Buy–sell agreement structure

Another consideration is the means for determining the purchase price, whether by formula, appraisal (including method of selecting the appraiser) or previously agreed to value, updated periodically.

Financial terms should be appropriate. Often buy sell agreements have down payments or installment arrangements which are simply unworkable; the owners and business simply do not have the liquidity or cash flow to support the required payments. Insurance can often help remedy this problem. Disability buyout insurance can lighten the load on a disability-triggered purchase, and life insurance can provide cash at death or a sinking fund, if a cash value policy, for other scenarios. The insurance should be arranged, as to owner and beneficiary, so as to be compatible with the structure of the agreement, which often is not the case.

Another issue concerns whether all entities should be subject to buy and sell agreements. What might be suitable for an operating entity, such as a manufacturing concern, may not be for a passive activity such as real estate subject to third party management, which could be successfully owned by numerous, unrelated parties.

All in the Family

Family-owned businesses entail unique considerations. A common scenario is that a husband and wife started a business with one taking a lesser role as raising children became a higher priority. Often not all of the children are in the business, giving rise to "inside" and "outside" children.

Planning needs to address the following:

- how will the business be conveyed to the future owners in the most effective fashion?
- how will mom and dad satisfy their income needs post-retirement if the business is not monetized through sale to a third party?
- how will the estate be equalized or at least equitably distributed between inside and outside children?
- how will a federal estate tax be paid on business holdings?

The answers to these questions often lie with the strategy of lifetime transfers and the bequest of the business to inside children with the outside children receiving other assets. Many of the strategies discussed in the estate planning chapter are useful in this regard (e.g., annual exclusion, lifetime exemption gifts, note sales, etc.). Ownership of stock by the succeeding generation, accomplished through lifetime transfer by gift and/or sale, may help them identify with their role as successor. It also shifts value out of the parent's taxable estate. But with resulting multiple ownership, a buy and sell agreement will be needed, carefully crafted to avoid tax problems unique to related party transactions. If mom and dad want to ensure continued control, they can simply retain a majority of the voting interest. Another approach is to issue non-voting interests, conveying an economic but not a voting right to both inside and, if desired, outside children. Comparable results can be achieved through managing and non-managing interests in an LLC. To further limit the growth of mom and dad's taxable estates, the business interest can further be separated into a growth and a frozen interest, sometimes referred to as common and preferred interests, as also discussed in Chapter 2, Estate Planning.

Yet another strategy, often referred to as "opportunity shifting," involves creating a new, yet often related, enterprise owned by the children. In this way, growth in value is organic to the child's entity rather than that of the parent's, which ultimately may have been subject to estate tax. Consideration should be given to making all gifts and sales, both for inside and outside children, into a well-designed trust rather than outright.

As to the question of income after retirement, mom and dad could look to other assets such as retirement accounts, and liquid investments. If company equipment or property is personally owned, fair market rent is another income source.

Salary can be continued for a reduced role such as board Chairman. Additionally, if the entity is a pass-through such as an "S" corporation, or LLC taxed as an "S" corporation or partnership, distributions can be made to mom and dad. Such distributions must be proportionate to all holders of the same ownership interest or class of stock. Issuing preferred stock if a C corporation or a preferred return interest in an LLC, for example, can justify a higher distribution rate. In any case, care should be taken to consider the potential burden on the enterprise of continued payments to support mom and dad's lifestyle and the succeeding generation's expectation of salaries commensurate with their new roles.

At some point, the matter of equitable versus equal treatment of inside versus outside children must be addressed. There is no right or wrong answer. The starting point is often to transfer the business to the inside children and other assets to the outside children. If there are not enough other assets to go around, additional capital can be efficiently created with life insurance. Where the business interest is of a size where it dominates by asset value or importance as a family institution, then it could be retained for the benefit of all children as well as future generations. Of course a sound governance structure will be vital to the long-term success of the enterprise, especially one exposed to the vagaries of family dynamics.

Following is an example of a structure for a large family-owned real estate business structured as a limited liability company (Fig. 4.2).

Finally, it is important that there is a periodic opportunity for the family to meet to discuss its goals, values, the role of the business in achieving these and any relevant business issues. Often, estate and business succession plans fail due to a breakdown in communication. An annual family retreat, supplemented with periodic conference calls, would be a means to help ensure that does not happen.

An important consideration in business succession is securing expertise to assist the future generations in their ascension to management responsibilities if still in a nascent phase when the senior generation passes or withdraws from the business. In addition to the existing team of advisors, the creation of an advisory board of industry experts can be helpful. Establishing an agreement with an expert to run the business for a period of time subject to discretion of a trustee may be helpful. Selection of a bank or trust company, with expertise in closely held businesses, is another consideration. Finally,

- Active children to be successor managers, or each individually, or as selected by a majority of members. Upon a managing member's death or disability or other triggering event, his or her interest reverts to non-managing member status

- Manager retains broad discretion in management duties, subject, however, to a majority vote of all members for the following:
    - proposed liquidation of greater than a specified percentage of entity assets
    - encumbrance of greater than a specified percentage (e.g. new debt)
    - suspension or reduction of distributions of greater than specified percentage over a given time period
    - redemption of greater than a specified percentage of ownership interest
    - admission of new members

- Maintenance of a board of directors, if desired, consisting of a minimum number of independent (i.e., non-family, non-employee) directors as elected by a majority of members

- Provision for reasonable compensation as determined by an independent consultant considering industry standards and the size and nature of entity properties

- Guidelines comparable to standard employment agreements regarding time and effort, non-competition and involvement in other business enterprises by managers

- Customary restriction on transfer of business interests for estate planning and for proposed transfer to a third party
    - permitted if transfer to family member or trust
    - if to non-family member, provides right of first refusal to entity and/or other owners
    - provision for determining price
    - terms of purchase

- Liquidity provisions for annual redemptions of up to a specified amount of shares, at manager's discretion

- Proportional income distribution to all members after manager compensation and other expenses

- Provisions for arbitration for dispute resolution

Fig. 4.2 Sample business succession structure

the importance of retaining senior employees whose continued employment is instrumental in supporting management succession, should not be overlooked. It is important to ensure they understand the owner's vision for family succession while themselves feeling recognized and adequately compensated. Such compensation would of course include salary and bonus but potentially a supplemental retirement benefit as well. Variously referred to as a supplemental executive retirement plan (SERP), non-qualified deferred compensation or "synthetic stock" plans, they can be powerful tools in key person retention and ultimate success of a business continuity plan.

No amount of planning sophistication is a substitute for children ill-prepared or ill-suited for their future roles. Mentoring is vital. As parents we do our best to instill the values and traits we believe are important and which contributed to our own success. But specific preparation in the technical and managerial aspects of the business and the freedom to fail occasionally are important as well.

The final consideration is how to pay the unavoidable estate tax after considering the various planning strategies employed to reduce it. These were previously addressed in Chapter 2. There is, however, another strategy available to owners of closely-held businesses, commonly referred to by its Internal Revenue Code: Section 6166. It provides for deferral of estate tax attributable to the closely-held business interest, if certain requirements are satisfied, including:

• business interest exceeds 35% of the adjusted gross estate and
• the estate must own at least 20% or more of the business entity or the business had 45 or fewer owners

The federal estate tax may be paid in equal annual installments over a period not to exceed 10 years and payment of the first annual installment may be deferred for up to five years (during which time interest is paid). The interest rate on the tax allocable to the first $1 million of business value (as periodically adjusted) is at 2%; the rate on the balance is 45% of the Federal underpayment rate. For real estate qualifying as an active business, 6166 is also available. Although the interest rate under 6166 is favorable, the fact that it is not deductible may result in an after-income tax cost that is not much different than a traditional bank loan.

Given the senior lien that the IRS holds and its attendant restrictions plus the burden of installment payments of a tax representing up to 40% of the business value, a 6166 election should generally be considered an estate tax payment method of last resort.

Not all transitions are destined to succeed despite our sincerest hopes and most determined efforts. Be prepared to make possibly the most difficult decision, which is that transition to the next generation is unrealistic and that another course must be pursued.

Sale to Employees

Scenario three looks like this: an owner or owners of comparable age desirous of retiring or at least slowing down and "taking some chips off the table" and where family members will not be involved. One solution is to sell the company to senior management. Ideally, the process is initiated several years in advance of the desired exit date by a sale or bonus of a small portion of the business. Done concurrently with an appropriate title, job description, compensation plan, training and mentoring, this can prepare the next generation for succession and success. At an appropriate date the balance of the business is sold. Of course the price should be based upon a quality appraisal. Terms may consist of an all cash sale (requiring the buyer to secure third party financing) or a cash down payment and installment note. Even incorporating all appropriate safeguards for the seller (for example, subordination and collateral requirements), this obviously is the riskier approach for the seller.

An alternative approach is to sell the business to all employees, not just the top executives (although they will likely still receive the greatest share) through the use of an Employee Stock Ownership Plan (ESOP). An ESOP is essentially a profit-sharing plan wherein the employer makes its contributions in stock in addition to or in lieu of cash. Its usefulness in succession planning is that the owner can sell his stock to the plan through what is known as a Section 1042 tax deferred rollover (if immediately after the sale the ESOP owns at least 30% of the outstanding stock). It works like this: within three months prior or up to 12 months after sale, the seller purchases "qualified replacement securities," often corporate bonds with long or indefinite maturity dates (e.g., 50 years). Capital gains, ordinarily recognized upon sale, are deferred until the bond is sold, or eliminated altogether if held until death due to the resulting basis step up. Cash can be generated by a margin or special purpose loan arranged through a brokerage firm or a commercial bank. The result is tax deferred or even tax-free diversification and liquidity for the seller, and a tax deductible purchase by the firm for the benefit of its employees.

Often the ESOP will not have adequate funds to purchase the owner's stock. A remedy may be to structure a leveraged ESOP. The plan can take out a loan, secured by the company. Plan contributions, up to specified limits, are deductible to the corporation, resulting in a pre-tax expense for both loan interest and principal.

ESOPs are not appropriate for all firms. As a general rule, they are available only to C corporations. It is generally not a suitable strategy where family members are intended successors (and hence, not discussed in Scenario Two), as company stock cannot pass to the account of related parties. The employee base and contributions need to be large enough to be practical. Stock value and company financial information must be provided at least annually, requiring an annual third party appraisal for a non-public company. Incidentally, if the stock value isn't growing, it's likely to create some employee discontent over time. And the company must offer stock repurchase for terminating employees. This all adds up to additional expense and complexity. But where it fits, an ESOP can be a great solution.

Sale to Outsiders

If a sale to insiders isn't in the cards, then a sale to an outside buyer may be the solution. This might be a cross-town competitor, a national firm, a strategic buyer, a private equity group, or the public, through an initial public offering or IPO. The sale could be for all or a portion of the business. If the latter, the question of retaining versus relinquishing control must be addressed. Business brokers, private equity firms, and investment bankers may play a role, depending upon the type of transaction. Of course, each specializes in size and industry.

Of particular importance with an outsider sale is readying the business for sale. Similar to preparing your home for sale, putting the best face on the business will be important for its marketability. Of course, earnings history is of paramount importance. But other considerations, such as condition of office, plant, and equipment, HR practices, accounting and information systems, are all important. Readying the business may take at least a year or two.

Is It Time Yet?

One thing each of the aforementioned scenarios share is the importance of knowing when "it's time." Whether it is age, health, level of energy, or passion, each of these factors contributes to the decision. Another consideration is financial need. While most successful entrepreneurs have a passion which inspires them to work far beyond when they need to work (think Warren Buffett), it is still important to know where one stands financially and the role the business plays in one's financial security. This is where the financial planning process comes in, as a useful if not essential prerequisite. In addition to acting as a catalyst for the introspection and self-examination, it will answer the question, "How much money do I need to extract from the business after tax in order to live my desired lifestyle?"

Questions to Consider

- Do you have a business succession plan? Is it in writing? When was it last reviewed?
- Based upon your planning "scenario", does it address the considerations and issues presented in this chapter?
- Are you aware of the impact that income and estate taxes will have on your plans?
- Have you decided when it will be time to "let go," to pass the reins to the next generation or to sell?
- Have you done the requisite financial modeling to know how much you must extract from your business, after tax, in order to sustain your lifestyle (and whether you should cash out or accept an installment or other arrangement)?

5

Asset Protection Planning

Creditors have better memories than debtors.
        —Benjamin Franklin, US author, diplomat, inventor, politician, and printer

The estate planning process may yield an advantage in addition to the desired distribution of assets with reduced administrative and tax induced shrinkage. And that is asset protection: techniques designed to protect assets from loss due to creditors and legal judgments. To be clear this isn't about efforts to avoid legitimate debts and obligations, but rather to potentially insulate yourself and your estate from frivolous or excessive claims, in some instances merely because of your wealth or visibility within the community.

The starting point is to reduce risks in the first place, both in your personal and business situation. Prevention, after all, is worth the proverbial pound of cure. Measures run the gamut from keeping a watchful eye on your teenaged child or grandchild's pool party for underage drinking, to sound employment practices in your business. Retaining a risk management consultant for a thorough audit of business practices is always a good idea.

Acknowledging that risks cannot be eliminated altogether, the next step in asset protection planning is maintaining adequate insurance coverage. A periodic review by a multi-line property and casualty insurance professional specializing in high net worth individuals and businesses is prudent. You can also insure some risks through a captive insurance company, as discussed later in this chapter. Insurance is fundamentally a contract for legal defense up to the limit of the policy, but for uninsured risks or awards in excess of policy limits, you're on your own.

© The Author(s) 2019
R. P. Rojeck, *Wealth*,
https://doi.org/10.1007/978-3-030-24497-2_5

As a matter of federal law, certain assets are protected. These include qualified retirement plans such as 401k, profit sharing and pension plans, and roll-over monies in individual retirement accounts (IRAs). In addition, state law may provide protection for your home equity, life insurance, and annuity products. Importantly, protection does not extend to divorce or IRS liens.

With the adage, "if you don't own it, they cannot take it away" as guide, the third line of defense is judicious use of business entities and trusts. For business-related risks, the most practical solution is to hold assets in a structure such as a corporation, limited partnership or limited liability company. For businesses where a separate tax status, bracket, and fiscal year are desired, a C corporation is often the entity of choice. Properly created and maintained, creditors' claims will not normally "pierce the corporate veil" and may hence remain at the corporate rather than shareholder level. However, individual or personal creditors can attach to the shares themselves. In contrast, a limited liability company may protect owners from business creditors and is normally not subject to attachment by outside creditors, as a charging order, in effect a lien against distributed income, is the usual remedy. And if the LLC chooses not to distribute assets or income to its members, the assets won't be available to the judgment creditor either. Hence, holding business assets in separate LLCs is often the asset protection strategy of choice. It is important to note that state law varies and is an important consideration in entity selection.

Referring back to the various estate planning techniques previously discussed, a revocable living trust, while important, may be of no benefit in asset protection. However when the first spouse dies, and a portion of the trust becomes irrevocable (i.e., the credit shelter and QTIP trusts), it may be an effective asset protection tool. A fundamental provision of an irrevocable trust is the so-called "spendthrift" clause that generally states that the beneficiary's interest will not be subject to their liabilities or creditor's claims or to assignment or anticipation. Irrevocable trusts, however, are generally created by one person on behalf of another in the process of gifts or sales from one generation to the next. So, the question is, how do you achieve this result on behalf of yourself, to protect your own assets?

SLATs, BDITs, and DAPTs

One approach may be a Spousal Lifetime Access Trust or "SLAT." As the name implies, a trust is created for a spouse by the other from their separate property or community property, which has been transmuted into separate property by a spousal property agreement. The annual exclusion and lifetime exemption may be used.

Children and their descendants are often included as beneficiaries as well. The spouse-beneficiary is commonly named as trustee and can control trust investments and make distributions to beneficiaries, subject to appropriate standards. Because the spouse-beneficiary is not the grantor (but rather his/her spouse is), and because of the spendthrift provision, trust assets should be beyond the reach of the beneficiary-spouse's creditors, as well as excluded from his/her estate for estate tax purposes.

It is possible for both spouses to establish a trust for one another. However, to avoid the reach of the Reciprocal Trust Doctrine, which could cause estate inclusion and loss of creditor protection, the trusts must be sufficiently different as to beneficiaries, dispositive provisions and other characteristics, so as not to be mirror images.

While there are many more details and considerations in the establishment of SLAT, in the right situation, a properly designed SLAT may achieve creditor protection and estate tax savings (Fig. 5.1).

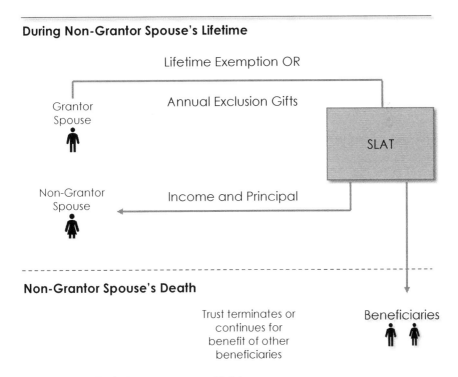

Fig. 5.1 Spousal Lifetime Access Trust (SLAT)

Another approach may be a so-called Beneficiary Defective Irrevocable Trust, or BDIT. It works like this: a trust is created on your behalf by a family member, most often a parent. Other beneficiaries, such as your children and their descendants, may also be included. You are named trustee, so you control trust investments and distributions, subject to certain standards. Because you are not the grantor and because of the "spendthrift" clause, trust assets may be protected from your creditors, and may also be excluded from your estate.

The method by which your own assets can achieve protection is by your selling them to the trust. And if they are worth more than the gift made when the trust was created for you (the likely scenario), the sale can be for a down payment (usually at least 10% of the value of the asset), and an installment note bearing interest at the Applicable Federal Rate. Because the trust is structured so as to be defective to you for income tax purposes (hence the name beneficiary defective irrevocable trust), you will recognize no gain on the sale (but will be personally taxed on trust income—a feature that can be extinguished at a later date, if desired). Since the note interest rate will likely be substantially less than the return on the assets sold, substantial value will be shifted to the BDIT over time. Of course if the asset is a business in which you are employed, you can continue to receive compensation. Income received by the trust may be distributed to you as a trust beneficiary.

There are a myriad of other considerations and technicalities associated with this strategy. But in the right situation a properly designed BDIT may provide asset protection and substantial estate tax benefits as well.

Still another strategy is a Domestic Asset Protection Trust (DAPT). With a DAPT you are the grantor, establishing the trust in one of several states with suitable statutes. An independent trustee of your choosing and whom you have the ability to replace (but not with one "subordinate" to you) can make distributions to any number of individuals you include as trust beneficiaries, including yourself. But you, as the grantor, are a "discretionary" beneficiary; the trustee is not obligated to make distributions to you. As the trust is irrevocable, trust assets should be protected from beneficiary's creditors, and judgments. As it is best that the assets be deemed located in the same state as the trust, assets are normally first transferred into separate LLCs (e.g., for securities, real estate, businesses) created in that state. LLCs are then transferred into the trust by gift (utilizing your lifetime exemption) and by sale for a note.

As with the BDIT, this strategy is also accompanied by numerous considerations and technicalities. An example is that most states with favorable

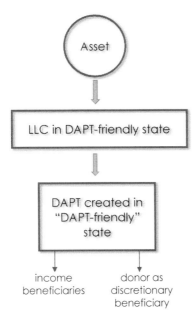

Fig. 5.2   Domestic Asset Protection Trust (DAPT)

DAPT statutes protect certain "exception creditors" such as divorcing spouses, alimony, a child entitled to child support, prior creditors and creditors whose claim arises after assets are transferred and before expiration of a statute of limitations. But as with the BDIT, a DAPT and its cousin—an Offshore Trust—may provide asset protection as well as substantial estate tax benefits (Fig. 5.2).

A final note: conveyances which have the effect of "hindering, delaying, or defrauding" a known or contemplated creditor will be treated as fraudulent and may be set aside (i.e., ignored) by the courts. Further, no strategy discussed is appropriate to all situations, nor is there any guarantee that they will be effective. But an asset protection strategy should be considered successful if it either induces a potential plaintiff not to file a lawsuit in the first place or encourages a settlement of the dispute for less than would otherwise have resulted.

Captive Insurance Company

If you ever wanted to be an insurance company executive or investor, the formation of a captive insurance company may be a means to succumb to its allure. Businesses are exposed to a multitude of risks from property and casualty loss, to liability claims, and more exotic risks, such as business interruption due to cyber attack. Traditionally, these risks were insured through commercial insurance companies. Now it is common for major corporations to create their own "captive" insurance company to insure some of these risks either as a means of cost savings, or to simply create insurance coverage not otherwise available while continuing to shift the risk of catastrophic loss to commercial carriers. Small, closely held companies may avail themselves of these same advantages.

The creation of a captive insurance company typically entails the following steps:

- An actuarial study
- A feasibility analysis
- Application for an insurance license with the appropriate state or country
- Entity formation as a C corporation or LLC taxed as a C corporation
- Capitalization

A captive may be domiciled outside the U.S. or in one of many states having applicable statutes. But the captive need not operate in that country or state. Fundamental to creation of a captive is that it must act as a true insurance company: pricing risks, issuing policies, collecting premiums, investing reserves, paying covered claims, financial reporting, regulatory compliance, etc.

The tax benefits can be significant, especially for a smaller "mini-captive" often used by closely held businesses. Premium payments are of course deductible as a business expense. For captives with gross premium income of $2.2 million or less (as adjusted for inflation), that premium income is tax-free; underwriting profits are also exempt from federal income tax. It pays tax only on income from its investment reserves which, if invested in dividend-paying stocks, may be eligible for the 70% dividend deduction from corporate income tax.

Creation of a captive, as with any entity, may give rise to planning opportunities. A captive may be owned by the children—or better still, a properly-drafted, irrevocable, multi-generational trust, such as that described in Chapter 2. If done at inception, gift tax consequences would be minimal. Appreciation in value (assuming that premium and investment returns exceed claims and administrative costs) may also inure to the trust gift-tax-free.

Obviously opportunities of this nature have invited taxpayer chicanery and significant IRS scrutiny. In one U.S. Tax Court case the court disallowed premium deductions the taxpayer had claimed concluding that the taxpayer's arrangement failed to distribute risk and that the taxpayer's captive was not a bona fide insurance company. The court pointed to a number of facts that it found problematic, including circular flows of funds, grossly excessive premiums, non-arm's length contracts, an ultra-low probability of claims being paid, and the captive's investments in illiquid assets.[1]

In summary, no financial plan should be considered complete without an asset protection plan incorporating sound personal and business practices, insurance, and careful entity selection.

Questions to Consider

- Have you had a recent audit by a risk management consulting firm?
- Has your property and casualty insurance carrier recently reviewed your risks and designed your coverage appropriately?
- Is your choice of entity structure suitable to your risk exposure?
- Would a captive insurance company be appropriate to your situation?

---

[1] *Avrahami v. Commissioner*, 149 T.C. No. 7 (August 21, 2017).

6

Life Insurance

I detest life insurance agents. They always argue that I shall someday die, which is not so.

—Stephen Leacock, comedian, teacher, writer and humorist[1]

Insurance is a concept that most of us have, at best, mixed feelings about. It's a necessary evil. Necessary, yes, as we understand that risks—natural disasters, and to a certain extent fires, floods, and accidents are out of our control. And of course if you're in business, the risks are magnified. Trading a few premium cents in exchange for dollars, should a claim arise, makes financial sense.

Life insurance often seems to elicit a visceral reaction, even though the ultimate event insured—death—is inevitable. I've occasionally heard the statement, "I don't believe in life insurance." Fortunately, life insurance is not a spiritual concept that simply requires "belief." It can be analyzed mathematically. So either it will make sense or it won't in any given situation. There are a number of uses for life insurance in financial planning for a wealthy individual. Before discussing them, let's start with a discussion of how life insurance is structured.

---

[1]Stephen Leacock, *Literary Lapses* (McClelland and Stewart Ltd., 1910).

© The Author(s) 2019
R. P. Rojeck, *Wealth*,
https://doi.org/10.1007/978-3-030-24497-2_6

Types of Insurance

Life insurance comes in two basic forms: "temporary insurance," also known as term insurance, and "permanent insurance," which comes in several varieties—whole life, universal life, equity-indexed universal life, and variable universal life. Temporary or term insurance derives its name from the assumption that the insurance will only be needed for a limited period of time. The most effective form of temporary insurance is level premium term insurance which typically comes in 5, 10, 15, 20, and 30 year durations. In the years following the end of the level period, the premiums increase substantially. In most cases, the policy will be convertible to a plan of permanent insurance with that company without having to provide medical or other evidence of current insurability.

Permanent insurance, as the name suggests, is for a long-term need. Long-term could be defined as the point where, economically, it is more advantageous to have purchased the permanent insurance. The crossover point is determined by comparing the term insurance premium with the permanent insurance premium and investing the difference in a "side fund" at a rate of return equal to the assumed earnings rate within the permanent policy, less applicable income tax. The crossover normally occurs between the 15th and 20th year. So if the projected need exceeds that, permanent insurance would generally be more appropriate. Also, term insurance is generally not available significantly beyond life expectancy, the point where 50% of the insured population is deceased and the other 50% survives. Therefore, permanent insurance may be the only practical solution for long-term needs, such as for the payment of estate tax.

The basic difference between term and permanent insurance is that with permanent insurance the initial premium is higher than the insurer's mortality and other costs, with the difference allocated to a cash value fund from which future charges will automatically be withdrawn when the current premium is no longer sufficient to cover them. The advantage of this arrangement, overlooked by many, is that cash values grow tax deferred as long as the policy remains in force. Therefore, the insurance costs are paid from untaxed earnings within the policy (i.e., pre-tax). The proof of this is that if a life insurance policy is surrendered, the gain (taxed as ordinary income) is determined after subtracting the premiums paid (which constitute the policyholder's basis) from the cash value. In effect, the cost of the insurance charges reduces or perhaps eliminates the taxable gain.

Following is a diagram depicting the basic concept embodied in permanent insurance (Fig. 6.1).

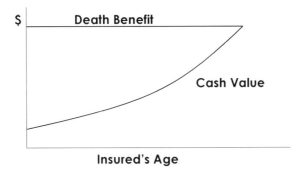

Fig. 6.1 Permanent insurance

This arrangement allows for a manageable insurance premium throughout an individual's life, no matter how long he or she lives—permanent coverage.

As mentioned earlier, permanent insurance comes in four different versions: whole life, universal life, equity indexed universal life and variable universal life. The primary distinction is in premium payment and cash value investment flexibility. A whole life insurance premium is generally fixed, although it may be possible through the addition of certain "riders" to lower or raise the base premium. In contrast, with universal, indexed and variable universal life insurance, the policyholder has premium payment flexibility to start with a low or high premium, skip and resume premiums (although, at the risk of a "lapse" in coverage if insufficient premiums are paid). As to investment flexibility, both whole life and universal life cash values are invested conservatively by the insurance company, generally in bonds and mortgages. However, in the case of equity indexed universal life, the credited rate is tied to the change in value of a stated index, typically the S&P 500 (an index of approximately 500 large U.S. exchange-traded companies), with a minimum rate of 0% or 1% to protect against years when the S&P 500 experiences a loss. In contrast, variable universal life insurance cash value is invested at the discretion of the policyholder in a variety of investment subaccounts resembling mutual funds. It is not unusual for an insurance company to offer 70, 80, or more different subaccounts representing most sectors within the stock and bond markets, domestic and international. This allows the policyholder the opportunity to capture potentially higher returns than that available with a whole life or universal life policy, although with accompanying increase in risk. Should the investments under perform over an extended period, there could be insufficient funds to sustain the policy and the policy would therefore lapse. Both universal and variable universal life policies are available with a no lapse feature—guaranteeing against a policy lapse if a specified "no lapse" premium is paid. Of course these and other features entail a charge, whether explicitly stated or inherent in the policy's cost structure.

Because future interest credits or investment returns are an unknown, it is important that periodic re-illustrations be obtained for existing policies. Such "point-in-time" or "in-force ledger" illustrations will take into consideration existing cash values as well as future planned premiums, earnings and expense assumptions to forecast policy performance. Such illustrations may reveal that the premium should be changed (increased or decreased) in order to sustain the policy as originally designed.

Policy Taxation

As an acknowledgement of its "social good," life insurance death benefits are generally received income tax free. And, as previously stated, cash value build up within a permanent policy is tax deferred as long as the policy remains in force and may be withdrawn on a tax-favored basis. There are, however, exceptions to the aforementioned tax treatment. Death benefits may become taxable if policy ownership is changed in a so-called "transfer for value" transaction. Additionally, cash values may become taxable upon withdrawal if "guideline premium" limits are exceeded, and cash value build up may be currently taxable under certain corporate ownership scenarios.

Life insurance proceeds will be includable in the insured's estate and subject to federal estate taxation, if certain "incidents of ownership" were retained. Hence life insurance policies intended to provide liquidity for estate tax payment should not be owned by the insured, but rather by a third party, such as an irrevocable trust for the benefit of the insured's beneficiaries. Finally, an unintended taxable gift can result in a three-party transaction—where the insured, owner and beneficiary are different individuals or entities.

So, needless to say, care should be taken as to ownership and beneficiary arrangements and ongoing policy monitoring.

Ways to Pay Estate Tax

So, with that by way of background, let's turn to some specific uses in estate and business succession planning for the wealthy individual. Perhaps the most common is to pay estate taxes. Even for those whose estate would not currently encounter an estate tax, if over their lifetime their estate is projected to grow to a greater amount than the inflation adjusted exemption, estate taxes will be an issue.

Obviously one could take the position "I don't care about the estate tax. It will be my kids' problem." But most people do care; they worked hard to accumulate wealth and they would like to preserve it. The fact that you're reading these words suggests that you are one of them.

In reality most people don't maintain the equivalent of 40% of their estate in cash to pay the estate tax because of the opportunity costs—what you could earn on it if deployed to better use (i.e., invested). So that option is moot. But even if that was the method of choice, it is not the cheapest.

Lacking cash, the executor would look to sell assets. Given that the estate tax return and the tax are generally due in nine months, that's not a lot of time to sell real estate and business assets. We've all heard of an estate sale and the notion it conjures up—a bargain! So it is not unlikely that assets are sold at discounted prices. Market conditions at the time of death can exacerbate matters. Asset prices, be they bonds, stocks, real estate, or a closely held business, are governed by the same valuation principles: discounted cash flow. So if cash flows and profits are reduced by poor market conditions and the discount rate is inflated by high inflation expectations or risk premium, the price is reduced. I'm thinking interest rates of 20% in the 1980s, courtesy of Fed Chairman Paul Volcker, whose mission it was to break the back of stubbornly high inflation; real estate after the Savings & Loan crisis of the late 80s/early 90s; stocks after the dot com bubble burst in 2000; and all asset prices following the financial crisis of 2007–2008.

Borrowing against an asset, whether it's a margin loan on marketable securities, a mortgage, or leveraging up a company's balance sheet, is an alternative that could be used in conjunction with available cash and asset sale. But it too has the effect of increasing the cost. Because interest must be paid on top of principal. That may be acceptable if the estate's assets could earn a return sufficient to cover it. But it has the effect of "leveraging up" the estate, which is precisely the opposite of what most individuals do at a certain point—de-risking the estate, paying down mortgages, eliminating cross-collateralization, etc. Re-leveraging the estate for the next generation by an amount of up to 40% of its value may not be a desirable outcome.

A counter argument could be that the discounted value at which an asset is sold, not a higher value, is its value for federal estate tax, eliminating the problem of selling at a discount. Mitigate, yes. Eliminate, no. If we assume an asset, originally valued at $10 million, declines to $8 million, the resulting estate tax at 40% would be $3.2 versus $4 million, an $800,000 reduction. But this still represents a loss of family wealth of $1.2 million ($2.0 million–$800,000).

The Economics of Life Insurance

So let's turn to life insurance. Depending upon age, state of health, whether an individual or joint life/second-to-die policy, and universal, indexed, or variable universal life policy is used, life insurance may represent a significantly less expensive approach when the premium, paid through life expectancy, is compared to the death benefit, as indicated in Table 6.1.

So for a 60-year-old male, life insurance represents a 70% reduction (37.6¢ versus $1.25 per dollar) in the cost compared to the likely alternatives: liquidation, or a borrowing. For a survivorship policy, the reduction is about 75% (30.2¢ versus $1.25 per dollar).

So from this analysis, one could conclude, "I don't have to 'believe' in life insurance. I can see that mathematically it makes sense." But there is still the question of: "Instead of paying an insurance premium, what if I had invested the money?" In answering that question, you first need to answer the question of "invest in what?" In order to achieve "an apples-to-apples" comparison, the investment alternative must share the same attributes as life insurance, namely: be liquid (death benefit is payable in cash from policy inception), safe (insurance can provide a guaranteed death benefit backed by the insurer's financial strength), and income tax-free (under federal and state law). So that eliminates illiquid, non-guaranteed assets, such as real estate, stocks, and closely held businesses from the comparison. That pretty much leaves tax-free municipal bonds which at the time of this writing are yielding about 2.5%.

Compare that to a return of 8.15% for the 60-year-old couple, representing the return on the premiums paid through their joint life expectancy. This is a taxable equivalent of 10.87% in a 25% combined federal and state bracket. Comparable results are achieved with other ages as well. As previously stated, results vary with age, gender, condition of health, and type of policy.

Table 6.1 Economics of life insurance

Male insured[a]			
Age	60	70	80
Cost per $1.00 of insurance	37.6¢	43.7¢	53.7¢
Male–female insureds[a]			
Ages	60/60	70/70	80/80
Cost per $1.00 of insurance	30.2¢	34.1¢	43.6¢

[a]Based on male standard non-tobacco and female preferred non-tobacco rates and representative universal life product guaranteed through age 100. Cost and rate of return calculation assumes premiums are paid annually through life expectancy based upon United States Life Tables as published by U.S. Department of Health and Human Services

In addition to comparing life insurance with other non-comparable asset classes, other factors are often also ignored in an analysis. One is leverage. Leverage, as everyone knows, magnifies returns as well as risks. Life insurance can be levered also. It's called premium financing. Banks and premium finance companies routinely finance insurance premiums, using the cash value, death benefit, and possibly other assets as security. Loan interest rates are usually a stated percent margin over London Interbank Offered Rate (LIBOR) or other index. Premium financing has the effect of enhancing the insurance IRR as it would any other asset.

And one final mis-comparison is in failing to acknowledge that a portion of the return on an asset being compared with life insurance is owing to the labor and expertise contributed by an active real estate investor or entrepreneur. Life insurance requires no such labor: You pay the premium, and the insurance company does all the work.

So, to sum up, does a wealthy person *need* life insurance? Of course not. It's the children's problem, and they can always liquidate or leverage up assets. But, if the question is posed as should a wealthy person *consider* life insurance, the answer is often "yes," because of the compelling economics. In fact life insurance is often thought of as its own asset class, possessing unique risk and return attributes. And as such, it should be carefully considered in structuring a comprehensive estate plan.

Other Uses

Let's briefly discuss some other uses for life insurance, all relating to the financial concepts discussed above.

- Leveraged gifts: A cash gift used to purchase life insurance immediately becomes the value of the policy upon the insured's death, and assuming normal life expectancy of the donor, provides a rate of return comparable to that discussed above. For example, a grandparent could create a trust for a grandchild exempt from the generation skipping tax, funding it with their annual exclusion of $15,000, which could be invested annually in a life insurance policy on their or their child's (i.e., grandchild's parent's) life. No gift tax, no estate or GST tax, no income tax!
- Leveraged gifts to charity: An individual could make a cash gift to charity to fund current operations as well as a life insurance policy as a future benefit. For example, a $1 million gift, with 50% allocated to a policy insuring the donor and her husband, both age 60, would generate a total

benefit of $2.2 million ($500,000 cash gift plus $1.7 million life insurance policy purchased with a single $500,000 premium). By the way, the $1 million charitable gift would generate a $400,000 income tax savings (assuming a 40% combined tax bracket) which if contributed to a trust for the donor's children, could fund another policy for approximately $1.4 million. Hence, $1 million ultimately generates over $3.6 million for charity and family.

Life insurance can also be a means to replace all or a portion of the value of an asset gifted to charity such as with the CRT and Retained Life Estate with Gift Annuity strategies discussed in Chapter 3, Charitable Planning.

- Buy/sell agreement funding. The economics of life insurance can be harnessed to fund a buy/sell agreement established for business succession or other purposes. If a cash value policy is used it may also serve as a sinking fund for a disability, retirement, or other lifetime buyout.
- Obligations and family income. Life insurance can indemnify a spouse upon the loss of wage earner, protect the company upon the death of a key person, repay a debt and fund re-purchase obligations under an Employee Stock Ownership Plan (ESOP).

Questions to Consider

- Do you know the amount of your estate tax liability today and what it is expected to grow to?
- Have you considered the economics of estate tax payment including its impact on the viability of your business interests?
- Is your life insurance correctly arranged so as to avoid income and estate taxation and facilitate its use for the purpose intended?
- Is your insurance periodically reviewed to insure it is adequately funded and performing as expected?

7

Investment Management

There are two times in a man's life when he should not speculate: when he can't afford it, and when he can.

—Mark Twain (1835–1910), American writer and satirist

Chances are, if you are reading this, you have already achieved financial success, having amassed significant wealth. You are likely financially independent, as defined in Chapter 1, by a significant multiple. You may continue to perform surgery, lead a public corporation, run a private company or companies, or develop real estate, because you love doing it. But your thoughts may be turning to the question of *preserving* capital, in addition to accumulating more of it.

Investing for wealth preservation is often different from how you built it. Building wealth almost always requires labor: often brutally long hours. It involves focusing on a narrow field of endeavor. And it often requires taking big risks, both business and financial. You knew if the venture failed, you could start over (perhaps you already have), and over again.

Wealth preservation, in many ways, is nearly the opposite. You typically rely on others' labor so you can pursue your favorite activities. It entails diversification. Risks are generally lower with a focus on return *of* your capital, rather than return *on* your capital. And while leverage may still be employed, it is lower. Your mindset is different: you don't want to start over!

This chapter will address the core principles of investing for wealth preservation through a diversified portfolio of financial assets. Let's start with a discussion of modern portfolio theory.

© The Author(s) 2019
R. P. Rojeck, *Wealth*,
https://doi.org/10.1007/978-3-030-24497-2_7

Modern Portfolio Theory

Modern Portfolio Theory had its genesis in 1952 with a University of Chicago doctoral student by the name of Harry Markowitz. His idea ultimately led to his receipt of the 1990 Nobel Prize in economics. Markowitz's insight was that instead of focusing on an individual investment position, the investor should instead focus on the return and risk characteristics of the entire portfolio.

Prior to his work it was understood that the return on a portfolio of investments was the weighted average of the returns on the individual components. Markowitz's discovery was that unlike return, portfolio risk was not merely the weighted-average risk of each of the underlying assets, but rather something less. He determined that by combining different assets: stocks, bonds, and other investment types into a portfolio, risk is reduced by a disproportionately greater amount.

In this context, risk is defined as the variability of the investment's return from the hoped for or expected return. Note that on this basis, risk could reflect better than expected performance as well as under-performance.

The mathematical process of determining the magnitude of the variation in an investment's return yields a measure known as "standard deviation." One standard deviation covers two-thirds of the returns. For example, for an investment with an expected return of 10% and a standard deviation of 18%, two-thirds of the time the return is expected to be between −8% and +28%.

Risk is often subdivided into "Systematic" and "Unsystematic" risk. Systematic, also known as undiversifiable risk, is that which is unique to an entire market of assets (sometimes referred to as an asset class). Examples of asset classes include stocks (large and small, domestic and foreign), bonds (corporate, government, and municipals, domestic and foreign), real estate and commodities. It is not possible to divest yourself of risk unique to an asset class. Unsystematic risk, on the other hand, is risk which can be reduced by diversification within and among asset classes.

The measure of a stock's systematic risk is its beta (represented by the Greek letter β). It is the extent to which a stock's (or mutual fund's) movement is explained by the market, usually an index considered indicative of the overall market, such as the S&P 500. A stock having a beta of 1 is expected to move in tandem with the market, both up and down. A stock with a high beta, say 1.5, would be expected to move up (i.e., outperform) or down (i.e., underperform) by 50% more compared to the index. The price of a low beta stock would rise and decline less than the index.

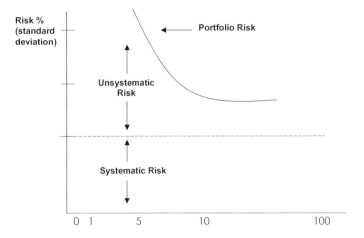

Fig. 7.1 Modern portfolio theory

Let's return to Markowitz's discovery and what it teaches us about how to construct a portfolio. As we learned, combining assets reduces risk. Risk reduction is owing to diversification. The amount of risk reduction is dependent upon the degree to which the assets move in the same direction at the same time, that is, the correlation of the assets' returns.

Graphically this would look as indicated in the following chart. What the chart is telling you is that the unsystematic or diversifiable risk can be reduced as you add more stocks and additional asset classes to the portfolio. And according to Modern Portfolio Theory, an investor isn't compensated with greater return for accepting unsystematic risk for just this reason … it can be reduced through diversification (Fig. 7.1).

A Model of Efficiency

Markowitz's model, when plotted, actually creates a diagram that looks like Fig. 7.2.

The vertical axis represents return, the horizontal axis represents risk. The curved line is known as the Efficient Frontier. The Efficient Frontier is simply a plot of portfolios that provide the highest return for each increment in risk.

Based upon an assumption that all investors are rational and that they would always prefer a portfolio that maximizes return for the risk, an

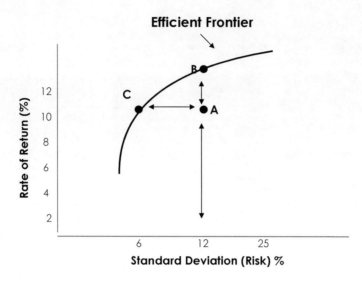

Fig. 7.2 Efficient Frontier

investor would never settle for a portfolio that was below the curve. Portfolio A, for example, is an inefficient portfolio because either it should be providing a higher return for that risk (such as portfolio B) or for the same return, it should be less risky (such as portfolio C).

Could a portfolio ever be above the line, meaning better than any other? The answer is … yes and no. By adding different investments, for example, foreign stocks to a portfolio consisting only of U.S. stocks, or real estate to one consisting only of stocks and bonds, or adding commodities such as oil and gas or precious metals, one could theoretically increase return and reduce risk, creating a superior portfolio. So, it would plot above an efficient frontier constructed of only two or three conventional asset classes. And that is the very argument for multiple asset class investing—blending many different types of investments to build a portfolio. However, if the efficient frontier had considered the additional asset classes, then all efficient portfolios would again plot on it. And in fact adding additional asset classes to the analysis, has the effect of causing the efficient frontier to move up and to the left…greater expected return with less risk.

Asset Class Diversification

At this point, you might be asking why shouldn't I just pick the "best" asset class and go with it? This investment approach has been labeled "put all of your eggs in one basket, but watch the basket *very carefully.*" Table 7.1 shows why not. It ranks the performance of seven different asset classes from best to worst each year over the past 20 years. What becomes readily apparent is that top performers one year are typically in the bottom a year or two later. This is one reason a blended portfolio will reduce risk and smooth out the investment ride.

What about just moving from one asset class just in time to exit the underperformer and capture the returns of the top performer, you ask? This is the age-old question of market timing, and it would be a logical strategy, if it worked. Studies have concluded that market timers need to be right 70–80% of the time to beat a buy and hold strategy; a nearly impossible task over the long term, especially when considering transaction costs and income taxes.[1,2,3]

Successful market timing mandates not just one but two correct "calls"—exiting the market or asset class before it goes down and entering before it goes back up, successfully repeated over and over again!

The Penalty for Missing the Market

Trying to time the market can be an inexact—and costly—exercise. This chart illustrates a $10,000 investment in the S&P 500 Index from January 1, 2002–December 31, 2017 (Table 7.2).

An attempt to quantify the importance of various factors in determining the return on an investment portfolio resulted in a landmark study entitled "Determinance of Portfolio Performance." Published in 1986 by Gary Brinson, Rudolph Hood, and Gilbert Beebower and updated in 1991 by Brinson, Beebower and Brian Singer, the study's findings were startling yet

---

[1]Robert H. Jeffrey, "The Folly of Stock Market Timing," *Harvard Business Review* 84, no. 4 (July–August 1984).

[2]William F. Sharpe, "Likely Gains from Market Timing," *Financial Analysts Journal* 31, no. 2 (March–April 1975).

[3]Jess H. Chua, Richard S. Woodward, and Eric C. To, "Potential Gains from Stock Market Timing in Canada," *Financial Analysis Journal* 43, no. 5 (September–October 1987).

Table 7.1 Annual total returns of key asset classes 1999–2018[a]

Ranked in order of performance from best to worst

Best→Worst	1999	2000	2001	2002	2003	2004	2005	2006	2007	2008	2009	2010	2011	2012	2013	2014	2015	2016	2017	2018
Best	Emerging Markets 66.84%	Real Estate 26.4%	Real Estate 13.9%	Comdts 23.0%	Emerging Markets 55.82%	Real Estate 31.6%	Emerging Markets 34.00%	Real Estate 35.1%	Emerging Markets 39.42%	Bonds 5.24%	Emerging Markets 78.51%	Real Estate 28.00%	Real Estate 8.3%	Emerging Markets 18.22%	Small Stocks 38.82%	Real Estate 30.1%	Real Estate 2.83%	Small Stocks 21.31%	Emerging Markets 37.28%	T-Bills 2.37%
	Foreign Stocks 27.30%	Bonds 11.63%	Bonds 8.44%	Bonds 10.26%	Small Stocks 47.25%	Emerging Markets 25.55%	Comdts 22.5%	Emerging Markets 32.14%	Comdts 14.5%	T-Bills 1.37%	Foreign Stocks 31.78%	Small Stocks 26.85%	Bonds 7.84%	Real Estate 18.1%	Large Stocks 32.39%	Large Stocks 13.69%	Large Stocks 1.38%	Large Stocks 11.93%	Foreign Stocks 25.62%	Bonds 0.01%
	Small Stocks 21.26%	Comdts 11.1%	T-Bills 3.4%	Real Estate 3.8%	Foreign Stocks 39.17%	Foreign Stocks 20.70%	Foreign Stocks 14.02%	Foreign Stocks 26.86%	Foreign Stocks 11.63%	Small Stocks -33.79%	Real Estate 28%	Emerging Markets 18.88%	Large Stocks 2.11%	Foreign Stocks 17.32%	Foreign Stocks 22.78%	Bonds 5.97%	Bonds 0.55%	Emerging Markets 11.19%	Large Stocks 21.93%	Real Estate -4.04%
	Large Stocks 21.04%	T-Bills 5.82%	Small Stocks 2.49%	T-Bills 1.61%	Real Estate 37.1%	Small Stocks 18.33%	Real Estate 12.2%	Small Stocks 18.37%	Large Stocks 5.49%	Comdts -36%	Small Stocks 27.17%	Comdts 17.2%	T-Bills 0.03%	Small Stocks 16.35%	Real Estate 2.5%	Small Stocks 4.89%	T-Bills 0.21%	Comdts 9.29%	Small Stocks 14.65%	Large Stocks -4.23%
	Comdts 7.3%	Small Stocks -3.02%	Emerging Markets -2.61%	Emerging Markets -6.16%	Large Stocks 28.68%	Comdts 11.2%	Large Stocks 4.91%	Comdts 16.4%	Bonds 6.97%	Large Stocks -37%	Large Stocks 26.46%	Large Stocks 15.06%	Small Stocks -4.18%	Large Stocks 16%	T-Bills 0.07%	T-Bills 0.05%	Foreign Stocks -0.81%	Real Estate 8.63%	Real Estate 8.67%	Small Stocks -12.18%
	T-Bills 4.64%	Large Stocks -9.10%	Large Stocks -11.89%	Foreign Stocks -15.66%	Comdts 8.9%	Large Stocks 10.88%	Small Stocks 4.55%	Large Stocks 15.79%	T-Bills 4.36%	Real Estate -37.7%	Comdts 23.7%	Foreign Stocks 7.75%	Comdts -8.5%	Bonds 4.21%	Bonds -2.02%	Emerging Markets -2.19%	Small Stocks -4.41%	Bonds 2.65%	Bonds 3.54%	Comdts -13.10%
	Bonds -0.82%	Foreign Stocks -13.96%	Comdts -16.3%	Small Stocks -20.48%	Bonds 4.10%	Bonds 4.34%	T-Bills 3.15%	T-Bills 4.73%	Small Stocks -1.57%	Foreign Stocks -43.06%	Bonds 5.93%	Bonds 6.54%	Foreign Stocks -12.14%	T-Bills 0.05%	Emerging Markets -2.60%	Foreign Stocks -4.90%	Emerging Markets -14.92%	Foreign Stocks 1.51%	T-Bills 1.39%	Foreign Stocks -13.36%
Worst	Real Estate -4.62%	Emerging Markets -30.71%	Foreign Stocks -21.21%	Large Stocks -22.10%	T-Bills 1.01%	T-Bills 1.37%	Bonds 2.43%	Bonds 4.33%	Real Estate -15.7%	Emerging Markets -53.33%	T-Bills 0.15%	T-Bills 0.14%	Emerging Markets -18.42%	Comdts -2.9%	Comdts -5.6%	Comdts -17.5%	Comdts -23.4%	T-Bills 0.51%	Comdts -3.92%	Emerging Markets -14.57%

[a]Data based on the following indices: **Large Stocks**—S&P 500; **Small Stocks**—Russell 2000® Index; **Foreign Stocks**—MSCI EAFE Index; **Commodities**—Reuters/Jeffries-CRB Index; **T-Bills**—90 day U.S. Treasury bills; **Bonds**—Barclays Capital U.S. Aggregate Index; **Real Estate**—NAREIT equity REIT index; **Emerging Markets**—MSCI Emerging Markets Index. Indexes are unmanaged and one cannot invest directly in an index

Table 7.2 The penalty for missing the market

Period of investment	Average annual total return	Growth of $10,000
Fully invested	9.92%	$41,332
Miss the 10 best days	5.03	20,873
Miss the 20 best days	2.05	12,566
Miss the 30 best days	−0.46	9330

Source Standards & Poor 500, December 31, 2017

Table 7.3 Determinance of portfolio performance

Activity	Contribution to portfolio return (%)
Security selection—active buying and selling of a security within an asset class	2
Timing—the decision to favor or avoid, i.e. overweight or underweight an asset class	5
Investment policy—the basic allocation between asset classes	93

confirmed what many had thought. The authors' database for testing was corporations' pension plans. The plan assets were separated into the three asset classes: cash, bonds, and common stocks. Their findings were as follows (Table 7.3).

These studies support the notion of the overriding importance of the asset allocation decision and the much lesser significance of market timing or even the selection of individual stocks or bonds in a portfolio.

Stocks

Jeremy Siegel, Ph.D., Professor of Finance at the Wharton School of the University of Pennsylvania, is noted for conducting exhaustive research into the performance and behavior of stocks. His data dates back to 1802. Over the 210-year period from 1802 to 2012, the return on common stocks has averaged 8.1%. This number includes dividend distributions. During that same period inflation averaged just over 1.4%, so the 210-year "real" (i.e., after inflation) return has averaged 6.6%.[4]

---

[4]Jeremy J. Siegel, *Stocks for the Long Run: The Definitive Guide to Financial Market Returns & Long-Term Investment Strategies*, 5th ed. New York: McGraw-Hill, 2014, p. 77.

What is noteworthy is the long-term stability of inflation-adjusted returns over the major sub-periods. Even since World War II, when the gold standard was renounced in favor of government-managed currency valuation—with ensuing inflationary results, the average real rate of return on stocks has been 6.4% per year. This is essentially the same as the preceding 125 years during which there was no overall inflation, according to Siegel.[5]

Siegel has also studied the returns on the stock market relative to other major asset classes, including U.S. Treasury bonds, Treasury bills and gold. Over the 210-year period from 1802 to 2012, stocks lead with a real (i.e., after inflation) return of 6.6%, followed by Treasury bonds at 3.6%, Treasury bills of 2.7% and gold at 0.7%.[6] This provides relatively convincing proof of the value of stocks in building and preserving wealth over the long term.

Risk and Return as a Function of Time

Long-term stock market performance can mask periods of extreme short-term volatility, the most famous being the Great Stock Market Collapse beginning October 29, 1929. During the ensuing three years, the stock market lost 89% of its value. More recently, we've witnessed combined losses of 34% in 2001 and 2002 and 37% in 2008.

But the longer the holding period, the less market volatility matters. Siegel studied holding periods of 1, 2, 5, 10, 20, and 30 years for the 210 years spanning 1802–2012. For each holding period, he identified the best and worst market performance. For the 210 one-year holding periods, one could have experienced a year when the market was down 38.6% or up 66.6% (remember that gains are part of the calculation of standard deviation, the basic measure of risk, though as a practical matter, they are far less objectionable than a loss!). But for ten-year holding periods, the worst performance was a 4.1% loss, and for all twenty and thirty-year periods during the prior 210 years, the worst performance was a positive 1% and 2.6% respectively.[7]

---

[5]Ibid., p. 82.
[6]Ibid.
[7]Ibid., p. 95.

Stocks and the Economy

Since stocks represent ownership in business enterprises, it stands to reason that the state of the economy will affect the profit-earning ability of those enterprises. The linkage between the economy and the stock market is well documented. Since World War II, the U.S. has suffered eleven recessions (a recession generally being defined as two consecutive quarters of declining gross domestic product) of which the average duration was about 11 months. The ensuing recoveries have averaged 58 months. Therefore in the post-war era the economy has been in recession about once every six years.[8] With few exceptions the market has retreated prior to the recession—on average preceding it by 5.4 months and beginning an upturn approximately 4.6 months prior to an economic recovery.[9]

Slicing and Dicing—Large vs. Small Company Stocks

Now that we have looked at stocks generally, let's take a look at some subcomponents of the market. When we think of the market, we frequently think of those giant companies that dominate American business.

But small firms have offered greater returns. Intuitively, this makes sense. Younger companies that are in a rapid growth phase as their products or services are introduced and are gaining market share have to offer the prospect of a higher return to attract investment capital due to their greater risk. Turning again to Siegel's research, in studying the period 1926–2012, the average annual return of over 4000 stocks was 9.67%. Stocks representing the largest 10% of companies returned 9.28% annually, while stocks of smaller companies generally returned more. In fact, those constituting the smallest 10% returned 17.03%. The largest 10% had a Beta (volatility relative to the market) of 0.95 whereas the smallest had a Beta of 1.38.[10] So, historically, smaller companies with their accompanying greater risk have provided a greater return. It should be noted, however, that the small versus large stock outperformance has not been consistent over time.

---

[8]Ibid., p. 232.
[9]Ibid., p. 234.
[10]Ibid., p. 177.

Slicing and Dicing—Value vs. Growth Stocks

While we are slicing and dicing, let's look at the investment characteristics of so-called growth and value stocks. Growth stocks are generally those with high price to book ratios. Their earnings are expected to grow at an above average rate relative to the market. Growth stocks are generally associated with technology but may be found in other industry sectors as well. Value stocks are most often those identified with utilities, oil companies, consumer staples, and finance. Returns on value stocks have exceeded those of growth stocks, and the difference has been most pronounced in smaller stocks. In studying the period 1958–2012, Siegel classified companies by size as well as their book to market value (a determinant of value versus growth status). He found that the largest growth stocks returned 9.38% annually, versus 11.94% for the largest value stocks. And while the smallest growth stocks returned 4.70%, the smallest value stocks provided 17.73% annually.[11] Numerous studies have attempted to measure and explain this phenomenon but with conflicting results. And it should be noted, the value-growth advantage varies over time.

Related to the notion of value vs. growth is dividend yield. During the same period, stocks in the highest quintile (20%) had an annual average compound return of 12.58% versus 10.13% for the S&P 500. And the second highest quintile returned 12.25% annually. Importantly, high dividend paying stocks also demonstrated a lower beta than the S&P index.[12]

Slicing and Dicing—Domestic vs. Foreign Stocks

The final slice of the pie will be comparing the returns of U.S. versus foreign stocks. Currently, foreign stocks represent about half of the world's stock value, so ignoring them would eliminate vast investment opportunities. Foreign markets can be further divided into developed and emerging markets. They can also be divided geographically. One could argue that the U.S. nearly 50% share of the world's market value still provides plenty of opportunity for the typical investor, especially considering that many large companies derive a significant share of their earnings from non-U.S.

---

[11]Ibid., p. 186.
[12]Ibid., p. 181.

operations. So why invest abroad? The principal reason is the diversification effect.

As measured during the period of 1970–2012, U.S. stocks price movement was only about 65% correlated to international stocks and for the sub-period 1988–2012 about 52% correlated to emerging markets.[13]

Factors

As previously mentioned, beta (β) expresses the movement of a stock (or stock portfolio) relative to the overall market (e.g. S&P 500). The theory behind it holds that in an efficient market, only by taking higher risk, as measured by beta, will investors achieve higher returns.[14]

In subsequent research, the outperformance of value and dividend-paying stocks as well as small company stocks, it was determined, was not well-explained by beta.[15] It is currently believed that beta may only explain about two-thirds of the performance; but when value and size are considered, the explanatory power rises to over 90%.

Research continues into these determinants of performance, often referred to as "factors." Numerous other factors have been more recently identified, with two considered significant: quality (i.e., profitability, earnings, financial leverage, and stock price stability) and momentum (i.e., stock price growth).

Bonds

As stocks are to ownership in a corporation, bonds are to lending money to it. A bond (sometimes referred to as a "fixed income" security) is merely an "IOU" that evidences the loan. But corporations aren't the only entities with borrowing needs. So do federal and state and local governments. Bonds issued by the federal government are referred to as governments or treasuries and those issued by state and local governments are referred to as municipals or munis. Treasuries and "general obligation" munis are backed by the full faith

---

[13]Ibid., p. 199.

[14]Beta is a component of the Capital Asset Pricing Model developed by William Sharpe and John Lintner in the 1960s. Sharpe received the Nobel Prize in Economic Sciences in 1990.

[15]Eugene Fama and Kenneth French are generally credited with developing a three-factor model for stock pricing which includes market risk, size, and value. Eugene Fama received a Nobel Prize in Economic Sciences in 2013.

and credit of the governmental entity or agency issuing them. The primary attraction of munis is their tax-free income. While corporate bonds are fully taxable both for federal and state purposes, and treasuries are taxable for federal purposes (although exempt from state income tax), munis are generally fully tax exempt from federal and state income tax if issued by the state of which the bondholder is a resident. For example, if you reside in California, its bonds will be tax-free. Yet, if you owned Ohio or New York bonds, for example, the Golden State would tax that interest. The fourth major type of bond is government agency bonds. These federally sponsored agencies, while not technically backed by the credit of the federal government, nonetheless are considered highly safe due to the presumption that the government would make good on its obligations (as it, in fact, did during the Financial Crisis).

As with stocks, most bonds are actively traded, post-issuance. Corporate bonds may trade on the New York Stock Exchange while governments and munis trade over the counter by banks and securities firms on behalf of their own accounts or clients. Numerous indices exist for tracking bond prices, such as those maintained by Barclays and Bloomberg (Table 7.4).

A Comparison

Attempting to tie our discussion of bond investing together, the following table ranks the major bond classes based upon total return (price change plus interest) for the 17-year period of 1998–2017.

Real Estate

If your business is real estate, you can skip this section. You already know all you need to know. But, if you're not an expert, you may want to read on.

If we look at the "market basket" of assets (i.e., what they represent of the whole of investable assets), it breaks down roughly like this: 50% bonds, 33% stocks, and 17% real estate. And while there's no requirement that your portfolio reflect the market, I believe it is a helpful point of reference. And indeed I find that except for those in the real estate business—where it often represents 90% of their wealth—it is underrepresented in a typical investment portfolio.

Table 7.4 Annual returns of key fixed income sectors[a] 1999–2018

BEST ↓ WORST

Rank	1999	2000	2001	2002	2003	2004	2005	2006	2007	2008	2009	2010	2011	2012	2013	2014	2015	2016	2017	2018
1	SHORT-TERM GOVT BONDS 3.41%	10-YEAR U.S. TREASURY BONDS 17.22%	INVESTMENT-GRADE CORPORATE BONDS 10.31%	INTL BONDS 21.99%	HIGH-YIELD BONDS 27.94%	INTL BONDS 12.14%	MUNICIPAL BONDS 3.51%	HIGH-YIELD BONDS 11.92%	TIPS 11.64%	10-YEAR U.S. TREASURY BONDS 20.47%	HIGH-YIELD BONDS 54.22%	HIGH-YIELD BONDS 14.42%	10-YEAR U.S. TREASURY BONDS 16.14%	HIGH-YIELD BONDS 14.71%	HIGH-YIELD BONDS 7.53%	10-YEAR U.S. TREASURY BONDS 10.57%	MUNICIPAL BONDS 3.30%	HIGH-YIELD BONDS 18.29%	INTL BONDS 10.33%	10-YEAR U.S. TREASURY BONDS 2.69%
2	HIGH-YIELD BONDS 3.28%	TIPS 13.18%	AGENCIES 8.31%	TIPS 16.57%	INTL BONDS 18.52%	HIGH-YIELD BONDS 11.95%	10-YEAR U.S. TREASURY BONDS 3.02%	INTL BONDS 6.94%	INTL BONDS 11.45%	INTL BONDS 10.11%	INVESTMENT-GRADE CORPORATE BONDS 18.68%	INVESTMENT-GRADE CORPORATE BONDS 9.00%	TIPS 13.56%	INVESTMENT-GRADE CORPORATE BONDS 9.82%	SHORT-TERM GOVT BONDS 0.39%	MUNICIPAL BONDS 9.05%	10-YEAR U.S. TREASURY BONDS 1.13%	INVESTMENT-GRADE CORPORATE BONDS 6.11%	HIGH-YIELD BONDS 7.03%	SHORT-TERM GOVT BONDS 1.60%
3	TIPS 2.39%	AGENCIES 12.18%	SHORT-TERM GOVT BONDS 8.23%	10-YEAR U.S. TREASURY BONDS 15.38%	TIPS 8.40%	TIPS 8.46%	TIPS 2.84%	MUNICIPAL BONDS 4.84%	10-YEAR U.S. TREASURY BONDS 10.03%	AGENCIES 9.26%	MUNICIPAL BONDS 12.91%	10-YEAR U.S. TREASURY BONDS 7.89%	MUNICIPAL BONDS 10.70%	TIPS 6.98%	AGENCIES -1.38%	INVESTMENT-GRADE CORPORATE BONDS 7.46%	AGENCIES 1.01%	TIPS 4.68%	INVESTMENT-GRADE CORPORATE BONDS 6.42%	MUNICIPAL BONDS 1.28%
4	AGENCIES -0.94%	MUNICIPAL BONDS 11.69%	TIPS 7.90%	AGENCIES 11.01%	INVESTMENT-GRADE CORPORATE BONDS 8.24%	INVESTMENT-GRADE CORPORATE BONDS 5.39%	AGENCIES 2.33%	AGENCIES 4.37%	AGENCIES 7.90%	SHORT-TERM GOVT BONDS 5.96%	TIPS 11.41%	TIPS 6.31%	INVESTMENT-GRADE CORPORATE BONDS 8.15%	MUNICIPAL BONDS 6.78%	INVESTMENT-GRADE CORPORATE BONDS -1.53%	TIPS 3.64%	SHORT-TERM GOVT BONDS 0.31%	INTL BONDS 1.81%	MUNICIPAL BONDS 5.45%	TIPS 0.86%
5	INVESTMENT-GRADE CORPORATE BONDS -1.96%	INVESTMENT-GRADE CORPORATE BONDS 9.08%	HIGH-YIELD BONDS 5.80%	INVESTMENT-GRADE CORPORATE BONDS 10.12%	MUNICIPAL BONDS 5.31%	10-YEAR U.S. TREASURY BONDS 4.51%	HIGH-YIELD BONDS 2.26%	INVESTMENT-GRADE CORPORATE BONDS 4.30%	SHORT-TERM GOVT BONDS 6.64%	TIPS -2.35%	INTL BONDS 4.39%	INTL BONDS 5.21%	HIGH-YIELD BONDS 5.47%	10-YEAR U.S. TREASURY BONDS 2.73%	MUNICIPAL BONDS -2.55%	AGENCIES 3.58%	INVESTMENT-GRADE CORPORATE BONDS -0.68%	AGENCIES 1.39%	TIPS 3.01%	AGENCIES 0.52%
6	MUNICIPAL BONDS -2.06%	SHORT-TERM GOVT BONDS 7.66%	10-YEAR U.S. TREASURY BONDS 5.42%	MUNICIPAL BONDS 9.60%	AGENCIES 2.59%	MUNICIPAL BONDS 4.48%	SHORT-TERM GOVT BONDS 1.93%	SHORT-TERM GOVT BONDS 4.18%	INVESTMENT-GRADE CORPORATE BONDS 4.56%	MUNICIPAL BONDS -2.48%	AGENCIES 1.53%	AGENCIES 4.36%	AGENCIES 5.17%	INTL BONDS 2.16%	INTL BONDS -4.56%	HIGH-YIELD BONDS 1.86%	TIPS -1.44%	SHORT-TERM GOVT BONDS 0.83%	10-YEAR U.S. TREASURY BONDS 2.13%	HIGH-YIELD BONDS -2.08%
7	INTL BONDS -5.07%	INTL BONDS 2.63%	MUNICIPAL BONDS 5.13%	SHORT-TERM GOVT BONDS 5.13%	SHORT-TERM GOVT BONDS 1.89%	AGENCIES 3.33%	INVESTMENT-GRADE CORPORATE BONDS 1.68%	10-YEAR U.S. TREASURY BONDS 2.53%	MUNICIPAL BONDS 3.36%	INVESTMENT-GRADE CORPORATE BONDS -4.94%	SHORT-TERM GOVT BONDS 1.28%	MUNICIPAL BONDS 2.38%	SHORT-TERM GOVT BONDS 4.82%	AGENCIES 1.51%	10-YEAR U.S. TREASURY BONDS -8.60%	SHORT-TERM GOVT BONDS 0.41%	HIGH-YIELD BONDS -4.93%	MUNICIPAL BONDS 0.25%	AGENCIES 2.06%	INTL BONDS -2.15%
8	10-YEAR U.S. TREASURY BONDS -7.74%	HIGH-YIELD BONDS -5.21%	INTL BONDS 3.54%	HIGH-YIELD BONDS 3.10%	10-YEAR U.S. TREASURY BONDS 0.18%	SHORT-TERM GOVT BONDS 0.92%	INTL BONDS -9.20%	TIPS 0.41%	HIGH-YIELD BONDS 2.65%	HIGH-YIELD BONDS -26.17%	10-YEAR U.S. TREASURY BONDS -10.09%	SHORT-TERM GOVT BONDS 1.65%	INTL BONDS 1.01%	SHORT-TERM GOVT BONDS 0.37%	TIPS -8.61%	INTL BONDS 2.68%	INTL BONDS -5.54%	10-YEAR U.S. TREASURY BONDS -0.14%	SHORT-TERM GOVT BONDS 0.41%	INVESTMENT-GRADE CORPORATE BONDS -2.51%

[a]Sources © 2018 Morningstar and Credit Suisse as compiled by Franklin Templeton Investments. **Agencies**—Barclays U.S. Agency Index; **Short-Term Government Bonds**—Barclays Capital U.S. Government 1–2 Year Index; **High-Yield Bonds**—Credit Suisse High Yield Index; **International Bonds**—Citigroup World Government Bond Index Non U.S.; **Treasury inflation-protected securities**—Barclays Capital U.S. TIPS Index, which is a component of the Barclays Capital U.S. Treasury Index; **Municipal Bonds**—Barclays Capital Municipal Bond Index; **Treasury Bonds**—Payden & Rygel 10-Year U.S. Treasury Note Index; **Investment-grade corporate bonds**—Barclays Capital U.S. Credit Index. Indexes are unmanaged, and one cannot invest directly in an index

Real Estate Economics

Investment in property actually provides potentially three benefits: current cash flow, appreciation, and income tax savings. The most fundamental way to classify real estate is undeveloped, also known as "raw land," and developed, otherwise known as improved property. Investing in raw land can be one of the most speculative forms of real estate investment. Unless it can be put to temporary use, for example, a parking lot or a driving range, your potential for return is solely from capital appreciation upon sale, which—depending upon location and direction and rate of development—is an uncertainty. Future marketability will be impacted by zoning, which determines the use by which the property can be developed by a prospective buyer, a process which has become increasingly slow and expensive nationwide. In the interim, you have carrying costs consisting of property taxes, liability insurance, and interest on the financing. Obviously the projected price must cover these interim costs plus a return for the risk involved.

In contrast, an investment in developed property generally involves less risk (that was borne by the developer, who converted the undeveloped parcel to its current state), and provides cash flow from tenant rent payments. With that, however, comes the responsibility of property management to sustain and increase those rents. Improved properties come in many forms and include apartments (including condominium conversion projects), office buildings, distribution and industrial facilities, shopping centers, hotels and others. Each has unique characteristics as it relates to appreciation potential, cash flow, marketability, and of course, risk. Incidentally timberland and farmland have emerged as investment opportunities and should be acknowledged here. However, as they are minor segments within the asset class, our focus will be on developed real estate.

A good measure of real estate performance is the NAREIT Index, produced by the National Association of Real Estate Investment Trusts (NAREIT). REITs are a means of investing in real estate. They are specialized forms of corporations that are exempt from corporate level taxes by satisfying a requirement to distribute 90% of their taxable income annually (though they cannot pass through losses that might otherwise shelter other income). Equity REITs buy apartments, shopping centers, office buildings, and other types of properties. Mortgage REITs, as the name suggests, purchase mortgages. Hybrid REITs invest in both. REITs may trade on a major stock exchange such as the NYSE and the NAREIT Index reflects the performance of these publicly traded REITs.

The by-now-familiar Table 7.5 that follows shows how the performance of various segments varies from year to year, as measured by total return.

Table 7.5 Annual returns by property sector[a] 1999–2018

Ranked in order of performance (from best to worst)

Best→Worst	1999	2000	2001	2002	2003	2004	2005	2006	2007	2008	2009	2010	2011	2012	2013	2014	2015	2016	2017	2018
Best	Apartments 10.73%	Lodging/Resorts 45.77%	Health Care 51.85%	Shopping Centers 17.72%	Health Care 53.59%	Shopping Centers 36.25%	Self Storage 26.55%	Office 45.22%	Health Care 2.13%	Self Storage 5.05%	Lodging/Resorts 67.19%	Apartments 47.04%	Self Storage 35.22%	Industrial 31.28%	Lodging/Resorts 27.18%	Apartments 40.04%	Self Storage 40.65	Industrial 30.72%	Industrial 20.58%	Health Care 7.58%
	Office 4.25%	Apartments 35.53%	Self Storage 43.24%	Industrial 17.32%	Shopping Centers 43.12%	Apartments 34.71%	Industrial 15.42%	Health Care 44.55%	Office 0.38%	Health Care -11.98%	Office 35.55%	Lodging/Resorts 42.77%	Apartments 15.37%	Shopping Centers 26.74%	Self Storage 9.49%	Health Care 33.32%	Apartments 17.07%	Lodging/Resorts 24.34%	Lodging/Resorts 7.16%	Apartments 3.09%
	Industrial 3.90%	Office 35.46%	Shopping Centers 29.89%	Health Care 4.82%	Self Storage 38.14%	Industrial 34.09%	Apartments 14.65%	Self Storage 40.95%	Shopping Centers -17.68%	Apartments -25.13%	Apartments 30.40%	Shopping Centers 30.78%	Health Care 13.63%	Health Care 20.35%	Industrial 7.40%	Lodging/Resorts 32.50%	Shopping Centers 4.56%	Office 13.17%	Apartments 6.63%	Self Storage 2.94%
	Self Storage -8.04%	Industrial 28.62%	Apartments 8.66%	Self Storage 0.56%	Office 34.01%	Lodging/Resorts 32.70%	Office 13.11%	Apartments 39.95%	Industrial -18.96%	Shopping Centers -38.84%	Health Care 24.62%	Self Storage 29.29%	Shopping Centers 12.20%	Self Storage 19.94%	Office 5.57%	Self Storage 31.44%	Industrial 2.64%	Health Care 6.41%	Office 5.25%	Industrial -2.51%
	Shopping Centers -10.71%	Health Care 15.10%	Industrial 7.42%	Lodging/Resorts -1.49%	Industrial 33.14%	Self Storage 29.70%	Lodging/Resorts 9.76%	Shopping Centers 34.87%	Lodging/Resorts -22.37%	Office -41.07%	Industrial 12.17%	Health Care 19.20%	Office -0.76%	Office 14.15%	Shopping Centers 1.86%	Shopping Centers 27.62%	Office 0.29%	Apartments 4.54%	Self Storage 3.74	Shopping Centers -4.96%
	Lodging/Resorts -16.15%	Shopping Centers 15.10%	Office 6.65%	Apartments -6.15%	Lodging/Resorts 31.69%	Office 23.28%	Shopping Centers 9.27%	Industrial 28.92%	Self Storage -24.82	Lodging/Resorts -59.6%	Self Storage 8.37%	Office 18.89%	Lodging/Resorts -5.16%	Lodging/Resorts 12.53%	Apartments -5.36%	Office 25.86%	Health Care -7.25%	Shopping Centers 0.95%	Health Care 0.87%	Lodging/Resorts -12.82%
Worst	Health Care -24.83	Self Storage -14.69%	Lodging/Resorts -8.63%	Office -6.82%	Apartments 25.49%	Health Care 20.96%	Health Care 1.79%	Lodging/Resorts 28.17%	Apartments -25.43%	Industrial -67.47%	Shopping Centers -1.66%	Industrial 18.41%	Industrial -14.31%	Apartments 6.94%	Health Care -7.06%	Industrial 21.00%	Lodging/Resorts -24.42%	Self Storage -8.14%	Shopping Centers -4.77%	Office -14.50%

[a]*Source* National Association of Real Estate Investment Trust Equity REIT Annual Return by property sector and subsector

Tax Benefits

Real estate is unique in comparison to other investments, such as stocks and bonds, as tax benefits can flow through to the investor if the property is owned directly or in certain types of business structures such as partnerships and limited liability companies. The tax benefits are derived from tax deductions for property taxes, utilities, advertising, routine maintenance, mortgage interest and depreciation. Depreciation is based upon the notion that the property declines in value over time due to wear and tear and general obsolescence. Generally speaking, residential property is depreciable over 27.5 years, meaning you would deduct 3.64% of the value of the structure (i.e. excluding the value of the underlying land) from income annually. Commercial buildings are generally depreciated over 39 years. Additionally, specific items (such as an air conditioning system) can be deducted over shorter periods based upon their expected usable life.

The results of these deductions may be that for income tax purposes, the property has very little or no income or even shows a loss while in actuality there is income after expenses. The ability to receive tax sheltered income enhances the attractiveness of real estate. Losses can be used to shelter income from other rental activities as well. Further, if the property is one in which you "actively participate" in the management, these excess losses may be used to shelter your earnings and other investment income. However, the annual deduction is limited to just $25,000, reduced by 50% of the amount by which adjusted gross income exceeds $100,000.

Regardless of whether you are actively involved, deductions not currently allowed may be suspended (i.e. saved) and then subtracted from your proceeds when determining taxable gain upon sale. Gain is calculated by subtracting from the sales price your "adjusted basis" (the purchase price, plus improvements, less depreciation) and selling costs. For federal tax purposes, gain due to depreciation recapture (i.e. gain recognition attributable to depreciation deductions) is currently taxed at 25% and the balance, the amount due to property appreciation, is taxed at up to 20% (and an additional 3.8% Medicare tax on investment income).

Under the Tax Cuts and Jobs Act of 2017, owners of a qualified trade or business structured as a pass-through entity (e.g. sole proprietorship, "S" corporation, LLC, partnership or trust) may be entitled to a 20% deduction from their qualified business income. This, of course, reduces their maximum tax rate accordingly on such income. For example, the top 37% rate becomes 29.6%. This provision applies to qualified REIT dividends as well (i.e. dividends not representing capital gains distributions). As with other provisions of the Act relating to personal income taxation, this provision is set to expire after December 31, 2025.

Commodities

The last asset class we'll discuss is commodities. Commodities represent the basic elements required for industrial production. They are the raw materials that economies consume in the production of goods used to sustain and improve our way of life. These commodities include precious metals, such as gold, silver, and platinum. Precious metals are used in more than just jewelry. They play a role in both the manufacturing process as well as in a host of finished products. Base metals include copper, lead, and zinc. The energy sector of course includes oil and gas. And agricultural items consist of cotton, wheat, corn, sugar, coffee, and cocoa.

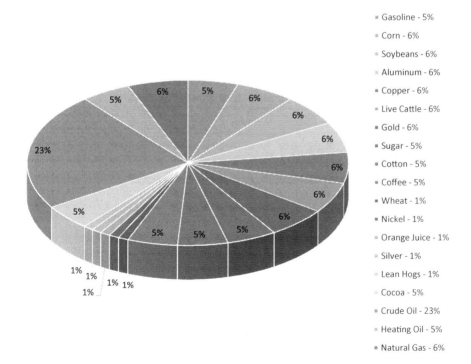

Fig. 7.3   Thomas Reuters Core Commodity CRB Index

As a result of their importance as an input to industrial production, they represent an investment opportunity. And because of their unique return and risk characteristics, they are considered an asset class—one which is potentially beneficial in creating an investment portfolio. As with other asset classes, the benefits derive from two things: investment return and diversification potential.

There are several commodities indexes. One of the best known is the Reuters/Jefferies-CRB Index, which is comprised of 19 commodity futures prices weighted as shown in Fig. 7.3.

Table 7.6 provides additional insight into the price behavior of various commodities.

Investing in Commodities

One approach is simply to invest in the stocks of companies whose business is the production or processing of commodities. While perhaps the simplest approach, it's not without its limitations. The first is the challenge of finding a "pure play," meaning a company who is exclusively in that one business. The best opportunities exist with oil and gas, coal or other mining companies. Agricultural commodities present more of a challenge as they may not be publicly traded or are part of a diversified food processing company.

One way to gain access to the energy sector is through an investment in the infrastructure supporting it: pipelines, tanks, rail cars, refinery and storage facilities. Likened to a "highway" for transport of crude oil, natural gas, natural gas liquids and refined products, income is generated by the "tolls" charged to transport them. Your return is derived from the tolls which are based on the volume of oil or gas transported, rather than the price of the commodity itself (though certainly influenced by it and the state of the energy industry). These investments are structured as master limited partnerships (MLP's) which trade publicly and must derive at least 90% of their cash flows from real estate, natural resources or commodities. MLP's are known for their high yield, currently over 7.5%, based on the Alerian index of 43 MLP's. Distributions, paid quarterly, may be sheltered due to equipment depreciation deductions. For this reason and other tax peculiarities, MLP's are appropriate for taxable rather than tax-favored retirement accounts. Of course, you can gain professional management as well as diversification by investing in a MLP ETF or mutual fund which, due to different tax treatment, might be suitable for your retirement plan.

An investment in an oil and gas program may represent yet another opportunity to participate in the energy commodity sector. Structured as

Table 7.6 Commodity price changes 1999–2018[a]

Best	2004	2005	2006	2007	2008	2009	2010	2011	2012	2013	2014	2015	2016	2017	2018
	Copper 41.30%	Natural Gas 82.55%	Nickel 154.45%	Wheat 76.65%	Gold 5.77%	Copper 153.14%	Silver 83.21%	Gold 10.06%	Wheat 19.19%	Natural Gas 26.23%	Nickel 6.91%	Corn -9.63%	Natural Gas 59.35%	Aluminum 32.39%	Wheat 17.86%
	Crude Oil 33.61%	Crude Oil 40.48%	Corn 80.88%	Crude Oil 57.22%	Corn -10.65%	Crude Oil 77.94%	Corn 51.75%	Crude Oil 8.15%	Natural Gas 12.11%	Crude Oil 7.19%	Aluminum 3.80%	Gold -10.42%	Crude Oil 45.03%	Copper 30.49%	Corn 6.91%
	Aluminum 23.52%	Copper 39.79%	Wheat 47.68%	Gold 30.98%	Silver -23.01%	Nickel 58.95%	Wheat 46.68%	Corn 2.78%	Silver 8.98%	Copper -6.72%	Gold -1.72%	Silver -11.75%	Copper 17.37%	Nickel 27.51%	Natural Gas -0.44%
	Silver 14.86%	Silver 29.20%	Silver 46.40%	Natural Gas 18.80%	Natural Gas -24.78%	Silver 48.16%	Nickel 31.47%	Silver -9.94%	Corn 8.00%	Aluminum -14.02%	Wheat -2.24%	Aluminum -17.79%	Silver 14.86%	Gold 13.09%	Gold -1.58%
	Gold 5.54%	Gold 17.92%	Copper 37.20%	Corn 16.72%	Wheat -30.99%	Aluminum 45.71%	Copper 29.96%	Wheat -17.82%	Gold 7.14%	Nickel -18.63%	Corn -5.52%	Natural Gas -19.11%	Aluminum 13.58%	Crude Oil 12.47%	Silver -8.53%
	Natural Gas -0.65%	Aluminum 16.19%	Aluminum 24.15%	Silver 14.65%	Aluminum -36.06%	Gold 24.36%	Gold 29.52%	Aluminum -18.95%	Copper 4.18%	Wheat -22.20%	Copper -14.00%	Wheat -20.31%	Nickel 13.49%	Silver 6.42%	Nickel -16.54%
	Nickel -10.29%	Wheat 10.33%	Gold 23.15%	Copper 6.14%	Crude Oil -53.53%	Corn 1.84%	Crude Oil 15.17%	Copper -21.35%	Aluminum 2.33%	Gold -28.04%	Silver -19.34%	Copper -26.10%	Gold 8.56%	Wheat 4.66%	Aluminum -17.43%
	Corn -16.77%	Corn 5.37%	Crude Oil 0.02%	Aluminum -16.70%	Nickel -55.37%	Natural Gas -0.89%	Aluminum 11.29%	Nickel -24.22%	Crude Oil -7.09%	Silver -35.84%	Natural Gas -31.21%	Crude Oil -30.47%	Corn -1.88%	Corn -0.36%	Copper -17.46%
	Wheat -18.44%	Nickel -10.12%	Natural Gas -43.88%	Nickel -23.56%	Copper -56.53%	Wheat -11.34%	Natural Gas -21.18%	Natural Gas -32.15%	Nickel -9.22%	Corn -35.96%	Crude Oil -45.58%	Nickel -41.75%	Wheat -13.19%	Natural Gas -20.70%	Crude Oil -24.84%

Worst

[a]Source Bloomberg and U.S. Global Research, www.usfunds.com

non-traded limited partnerships, they typically involve "developmental" drilling—new wells in proven oil fields. Cash distributions, sheltered by the oil and gas depletion allowance, can be significant, but are highly dependent on the direction of oil and gas prices.

Let's turn to another approach, investing directly in the commodity itself. This is a practical method for precious metals, such as gold and silver, as they are readily available in the form of coins and bars. Further, because they have a high value relative to their size, they are easily stored and safeguarded (e.g. in a bank safe deposit box). But what about agricultural commodities and oil, for example? Unless you have a sizeable barn or oil tank farm, you may want to take another approach.

Enter the futures contract. Commodity futures contracts are standardized contracts traded on domestic and foreign commodities exchanges, which call for the future delivery of specified quantities of commodities at a specified time, place, and price, as determined at the time of purchase or sale of the contract. The contract is between a buyer and seller. The seller closes out his position by buying back the same contract type and quantity. The original buyer closes out his position by selling the same contract type and quantity. So, few contracts ever go to final delivery. For example, the futures contract for Light Sweet Crude Oil on the New York Mercantile Exchange represents 1000 barrels and the grade or quality stipulates such things as sulfur content and origin. A trader who thinks that crude oil prices will fall will sell the futures contract in the hope of buying it back at a lower price for a profit (taking a "short" position). A trader who thinks prices will rise will buy the contract in the hope of selling the contract at a higher price later for a profit (taking a "long" position). The ability to sell a contract to potentially profit from a decline in price provides potential for profit even in declining markets. Of course, should the market for crude oil not move in the desired direction the trader will lose on his position. Future contracts generally expire quarterly, requiring a new contract in order to maintain the desired position.

In addition to traditional commodities, contracts on financial futures such as stock indices, currencies and interest rates exist. Currency contracts represent a commitment to buy or sell an underlying currency. The ultimate gain or loss is equal to the difference between the value of the contract at the onset and the value of the contract at the settlement date.

A variation on a futures contract is a forward contract, the distinction being that forwards are not traded on an organized futures exchange. Instead, they trade primarily in the so-called interbank market dominated by the world's major commercial and investment banks. This is essentially an over-the-counter network of trading relationships among worldwide participants. In addition to traditional commodities, there is an active currency market for virtually all major currencies.

The last vehicle we'll discuss is options. Options are contracts that give buyers the right (but not the obligation) to buy or to sell a given commodity. They come in two basic forms. A call option gives the buyer the right to buy a commodity; a put option gives the buyer the right to sell that commodity. An investor may also sell a put or call option. Options trade both on exchanges as well as over-the-counter.

Commodity investing involves some unique income tax treatment. Futures contracts which trade on US and certain foreign exchanges are taxed under a "mark-to-market" system. This provides that any unrealized profit or loss on such positions which are open as of the end of the year will be treated as if such profit or loss had been realized. Generally speaking, 60% of the net gain or loss is treated as long-term capital gain or loss, and the remaining 40% of such net gain or loss is treated as short-term gain or loss. Losses are only deductible to the extent of an investor's basis in the partnership, which generally consists of the original investment plus profits not distributed.

Principles of Portfolio Construction

With the foregoing as background, let's discuss the process of building and managing an investment portfolio. The portfolio construction process requires numerous inputs, including:

* Risk tolerance
* Investment timeframe/horizon
* Objective for return, including current income
* Liquidity needs
* Income tax rate
* Simplicity and transparency preferences
* Environmental, social, and governance considerations

While the process is mathematically driven, incorporating the concepts of risk, return, and correlation previously discussed, it also involves a significant element of art. For example, while sophisticated tools have been developed to assess an investor's risk tolerance—that level of volatility just before you say "I've had enough, I want out"—the judgment of the financial planner is important as well. Client temperament, previous investment experience and other considerations all bear on the appropriate risk level of the portfolio and must be considered.

Furthermore, the inputs will differ based upon the nature of the portfolio, even if for the same individual. For example, a portfolio constructed for a married couple held in their revocable trust would likely be different than for their roll-over IRA or for an investment account held in their irrevocable "dynasty" trust or for their private foundation.

As previously discussed, the objective in portfolio construction is to achieve a portfolio which is on the efficient frontier, meaning that potential return is maximized consistent with investor risk tolerance (or risk is minimized for an expected return). A mathematical model known as a portfolio optimizer is used for this purpose. Following is a risk-return efficient portfolio, product of a portfolio optimizer. Again, a planner's judgment may be

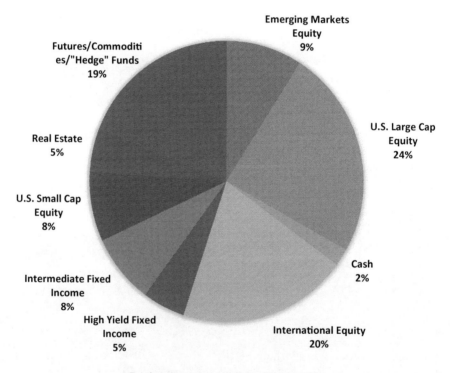

Projected Annual Return 7.7%
Projected Standard Deviation 13.8%

Fig. 7.4 Sample portfolio

applied to adjust an allocation for better alignment with the aforementioned portfolio construction considerations (e.g., a larger allocation to real estate or smaller allocation to futures/commodities and hedge funds). And of course projected return and risk are just that: projections, as there can be no guarantee that projected results will be achieved (Fig. 7.4).

Implementation

Once an allocation is achieved, the next step is to decide how the allocation will be implemented. A matter of ongoing debate is whether the portfolio should be passive or active or a combination thereof. Passive management relies on an index such as the S&P 500 for U.S. large company stocks, the Russell 2000 for U.S. small companies, or Morgan Stanley EAFE for international stocks. Indexing can be achieved through a separate account (i.e. portfolio of individual securities managed for a client), mutual fund, or exchange-traded fund (ETF). As studies have shown that active managers underperform their index, measured over extended periods, a strong argument can be made for a passive management approach.[16,17] A related issue is cost, the major contributor to underperformance. For example, the average fee for an actively managed stock mutual fund is 0.80% (8/10th of 1%), whereas an ETF tracking the S&P 500 can be had for 0.10% (10 basis points or 1/10th of 1%) or less.

Often, a portfolio is constructed with a combination of both passive and active management. Index funds can be used to implement "core" holdings—broad allocations to equity markets, both domestic and foreign. Active managers can be incorporated with the objective of enhancing return and/or reducing risk, especially in selected stock and bond market segments.

One measure of risk adjusted return is "alpha"—a measure of the difference between a fund's actual return and its expected return given its level of risk. As we've previously discussed, risk is measured by "beta", which reflects the extent to which the fund moves in tandem with a market index, such as the S&P 500 (as such it measures "co-variance" risk). A fund with a beta of 1.00 has volatility equal to that of the S&P 500; a beta of 0.80 suggests that the fund would vary up, or down, 80% as much as the S&P 500. A fund with an alpha of 2 would reflect that the fund out performed by 2% the

---

[16]Mark M. Carhart, "On Persistence in Mutual Fund Performance," *Journal of Finance* 52, no. 1 (March 1997).

[17]Mark M. Carhart, Jennifer N. Carpenter, Anthony W. Lynch, and David K. Musto, "Mutual Fund Survivorship," *The Review of Financial Studies* 15, no. 5 (2002).

expected return taking into account the movement of the market and the beta of the fund. The higher the alpha, the more "value" the manager's skill has added.

A core holding for the bond allocation is typically achieved by purchasing individual bonds of increasing maturities—from one to ten years for example. Known as a "bond ladder," it will reduce exposure to interest rate risk (principal loss as interest rates rise), if the bonds are held to maturity. Bond ladders can be constructed from the various types previously discussed. An active bond manager could be added to take advantage of pricing anomalies and other factors, possibly investing in high yield or foreign bonds.

Another consideration in portfolio construction is emphasis on factors that drive performance, such as those previously discussed. Emphasizing value versus growth stocks is an example. Factors can be captured through separately managed accounts of individual stocks as well as mutual funds and ETFs. A relatively new concept known as "Smart Beta" has gained recognition of late. It lies somewhere between index investing and active management, and is based on the notion that while stock picking is a fool's errand, it's possible to outperform by screening for certain factors such as value (vs growth), company size (emphasizing smaller companies), quality and profitability, price momentum, and others. The simplest example might be a mutual fund employing an equal versus market capitalization weighting of stocks comprising the S&P 500 index. This will tend to emphasize smaller value companies rather than the largest technology stocks. Research supports the notion that this and other smart Beta or factor strategies outperform a pure indexing approach.

Another consideration in building a portfolio is "ESG": Environmental, Social, and Governance (formerly known as Socially Responsible Investing) considerations. Consideration of how a company behaves, its impact on the environment and society establish additional screens or standards for an investment's inclusion in the portfolio. Typical screens include:

Environmental Screens

- Fossil Fuels
- Carbon Intensity
- Environmental Controversies
- Genetic Engineering
- Nuclear Power

Social Screens

* Alcohol and Firearms
* Animal Welfare
* Global Weapons Producers
* Human Rights
* Tobacco

There is a growing body of evidence that shows that high ESG-scoring companies actually produce more reliable earnings and outperform the market.[18]

In addition to publicly traded securities, active management can also incorporate private equity and private debt as a means to achieve further diversification and the potential for higher return and lower correlation with other asset classes, but often with greater risk.

Private equity firms typically invest in smaller firms, though they may also seek take-over opportunities in more mature publicly traded companies that—with the infusion of capital and new management—represent turn-around opportunities. Private debt is an alternative to bank funding to smaller and mid-market firms, providing a source of capital for growth as well as for buy-outs. Both private equity and debt investments are typically structured as limited partnerships, entailing minimum investments of $250,000 to $1 million or more, generally have 3–5 year or longer investment horizons, and significant restrictions on redemption or transfer.

Another strategy which often plays a role in a portfolio for a high net worth investor is a hedge fund. While traditional investments, such as stocks and bonds, provide an opportunity for investment gain over time, that result can be interrupted by periods of negative returns. Investment managers who beat their index or benchmark, could still post a negative return if the market, as measured by the S&P 500 index, for example, is down.

In contrast, a hedge fund generally seeks to achieve absolute return, meaning a positive return, regardless of the direction of the market. Hedge fund managers employ various strategies in pursuit of their absolute return objective. They may invest on margin, which is simply borrowing to

---

[18]Gunnar Friede, Timo Busch, and Alexander Bassen, "ESG and Financial Performance: Aggregated Evidence from More Than 2000 Empirical Studies," *Journal of Sustainable Finance & Investment* 5, no. 4 (October 2015).

purchase securities. This has the effect of leveraging or enhancing returns because larger investments can be controlled with a much smaller sum. Another is short-selling. This is essentially buying low and selling high in reverse.

Hedge funds can also be characterized by differing investment styles such as long/short equity, event driven (e.g., bankruptcies, mergers, reorganizations and spin-offs), relative value (e.g., perceived mis-pricings within different securities—the stock and convertible bond of the same company), global macro (e.g. mis-pricings between countries and across asset classes) and managed futures.

Hedge funds have not always lived up to these expectations; the most egregious example perhaps was the demise of Long Term Capital Management resulting from the fallout of the Russian bond crises in 1998 when that government defaulted on its debt. But, you really need not look further than 2008 to see how hedge funds have performed in a deep bear market. While many achieved their objective of providing a positive return, in a year when the market, measured by the S&P, declined 37%, the average hedge fund posted an 18% loss, according to industry source Hedge Fund Research. While a significant improvement, it was still not the "absolute return" most hedge fund investors were expecting.

Traditionally, they have been structured as limited partnerships with investment minimums and restrictions similar to private equity investments as described above. More recently, hedge fund-like investments have been offered as mutual funds.

On-Going Management

Once the allocation is set, a portfolio benchmark return can be established, against which portfolio performance can be measured. Portfolio objectives, risk tolerance, income tax status, liquidity need, and other considerations, and resulting asset allocation, are memorialized in a document known as an Investment Policy Statement. An IPS is the investment advisor's "manual" for how to manage the portfolio. Virtually all institutional money: public charities, endowments, and pension plans are governed by an IPS. Your portfolio should be too. Following is an outline for a well-written document (Fig. 7.5).

I.   Purpose

II.   Statement of Objectives
    A. Background
    B. Time Horizon
    C. Tax Policy
    D. Liquidity Needs
    E. Constraints
    F. Risk Tolerance

III.   Asset Allocation and Modeled Return
    A. Updated Allocations
    B. Rebalancing Procedures

IV.   Duties and Responsibilities
    A. Investment Advisor
    B. The Custodian
    C. The Client

V.   Advisor Philosophy

VI.   Investment Selection

VII.   Investment Monitoring
    A. Benchmarks
    B. Performance Objectives
    C. Watch List Criteria
    D. Replacement of an Investment

VIII. Identifying, Evaluating, and Containing Costs

IX.   Investment Policy Review

X.   Adoption

XI.   Appendix A: Asset Allocation

XII.   Appendix B: Asset Class Benchmarks

XIII. Appendix C: Due Diligence Criteria

Fig. 7.5 Sample Investment Policy Statement Outline (*Source* Adapted from "Sample Investment Policy Statement – Retirement Plan 3(38)" by Fi360, Inc., 2018. Copyright 2018 by Fi360, Inc. Adapted with permission)

Questions to Consider

This brings us to the conclusion of our investment discussion, and with that I pose the following questions for your consideration:

- Is your portfolio structured to maximize potential return consistent with your tolerance of risk (or minimize risk consistent with your return objective)?
- Is the impact of income taxes being minimized through active tax loss harvesting and other strategies?

- Are you minimizing expenses?
- Are your active managers adding value on a risk-adjusted basis (i.e., generating alpha)?
- Do you have an Investment Policy Statement for each of your portfolios (e.g., revocable trust, private foundation, irrevocable trust[s])?

Time for a Family Office?

You may be asking yourself, "Do I need a family office?" Or more fundamentally, "What is a family office?" The family office concept has existed since at least the late nineteenth century; it is believed the first in the U.S. was formed by the Rockefeller family to manage the oil magnate's wealth. As stated in their 2016 Family Office Guide, accounting firm Ernst & Young reports that there were at least 10,000 family offices worldwide and at least half of those were established within the last 15 years.

Many family offices have garnered notice for their investment activities. Recently, several high profile hedge funds have returned investor monies and converted to a private family office, tending to the former manager's personal wealth. Those that only manage money for descendants of a common ancestor within 10 generations are exempt from registration with the Securities Exchange Commission.

In addition to investing in publicly traded securities (e.g. exchange-traded stocks and bonds), family offices often invest in private debt, equity and real estate funds sponsored by private equity firms and hedge funds. Increasingly, they are investing directly in such opportunities, either on their own, or with other family offices, to acquire farmland, seed a hedge fund or buy entire companies.

It's been said "If you've seen one family office … you've seen one family office." While they are nearly as diverse as the families they serve there are two basic types: single family offices and multiple family offices. In addition to investment management services, they may offer business and property management (including residences and yachts), accounting and cash management, estate and philanthropic planning, income tax planning and preparation, family governance, financial and investment education, and concierge services such as managing household staff, travel and other lifestyle activities. Estimates of minimum investable assets range from $100 million to $250 million or more for a full service single family office with its own investment professionals and other staff. Multi family offices may require only $25 million or even less, though they may not provide the full range of services mentioned.

Financial institutions offer certain family office services either in support of a family office, or directly to high net worth individuals and families. Such services are also offered by financial planners, coordinating the activities of a team of professionals and service providers (e.g., CPAs, attorneys, trust companies, family consultants, etc.).

Perhaps your needs can be met by a competent team of financial, tax, and legal advisors along with a reliable bookkeeper to pay your bills and keep your personal records in order. But as your affairs grow, along with the number of family members and generations whose wealth you wish to manage and protect, choosing the right family office model will be an important decision.

8

Income Tax Planning

The art of taxation consists in so plucking the goose as to obtain the largest amount of feathers with the least amount of hissing.
—Jean Baptiste Colbert (1619–1683), *French Statesman*

As the saying goes, only two things in life are certain: death and taxes. Which of the two is most objectionable is open to debate. Few of us dispute the necessity of income taxes as a means to pay for services that local, state and federal governments provide. The argument is, which services and at what price. Assuming you're in the top federal bracket, you've likely been working about five months each year to pay your income tax. If you live in a state with a high state income tax, you can add another month and a half.

This chapter is not intended to be an all-encompassing discussion of federal and state income taxation, an undertaking requiring volumes many times the size of this book. Rather the goal is to provide an overview of practical income tax planning opportunities for wealthy individuals.

A helpful starting point in this discussion is the Federal Income Tax return itself, Form 1040. The basic format is you begin with your income from its various sources, subtract "above the line" deductions to arrive at your adjusted gross income, then subtract certain itemized deductions to arrive at your taxable income. Finally, you apply your tax rate, subtracting available tax credits, and adding any additional taxes, to arrive at the tax due. So, it stands to reason that reducing reportable income and increasing deductions is a good thing when it comes to reducing your income tax.

© The Author(s) 2019
R. P. Rojeck, *Wealth*,
https://doi.org/10.1007/978-3-030-24497-2_8

The way I view it, there are four basic categories of tax strategies:

- Deferral—postponing when you must legally report income so that you can benefit by either using it or investing it in the meantime. Even though you ultimately report the income, the "time value" of money can work to your advantage.
- Converting—changing the form of the income to that taxed more favorably.
- Diverting—shifting income to another tax paying entity or person taxed at a lower rate.
- Deductions—reducing your reported income and thus the amount subject to income tax.

Many of the strategies are complex, involving numerous technicalities regarding qualification and structure. But let's take a high level look at each.

Deferral

The first category is that of deferral. It's been said, "Pay tax on what you take and not on what you make." If you are not currently spending your income, why pay taxes on it? The power of this concept is significant and is magnified as the period of accumulation is increased. Let's look at a simple example of an individual in a 50% tax bracket, investing $100,000 annually, with an 8% pre-tax investment return (Table 8.1).

As you can see from this example, avoiding current income taxation of investment earnings over the 20-year period results in additional accumulation of nearly $1.6 million or 54% of the currently taxed sum. The ultimate value of the tax-deferral is a function of the length of continued deferral and the investor's tax bracket upon withdrawal.

Table 8.1 Advantage of tax deferral (cumulative value)

Years	Annual investment	Investment return[a]		Deferral
		8%	4%	Advantage
1	100,000	108,000	104,000	4000
5	100,000	586,660	541,632	45,028
10	100,000	1,448,656	1,200,611	248,045
15	100,000	2,715,211	2,002,359	712,852
20	100,000	4,576,196	2,977,808	1,598,388

[a]Assumes 8% pre-tax hypothetical return and a 50% combined federal and state income tax bracket, yielding a 4% after tax return

Earned Income

Retirement Plans

Qualified retirement plans are perhaps the most common strategies for tax deferral. The term "qualified" means the plan meets certain requirements, allowing participants and plan sponsors to enjoy income tax, creditor protection, and other benefits. Examples include 401K, profit sharing and defined benefit pension plans. Earnings grow tax deferred until withdrawn (except for Roth plans, which are never taxed if you follow the rules). Additionally, contributions are tax deductible (again, except for Roth plans). Hence, these plans actually fall into two of the four tax planning strategies: Defer and Deduct.

What if you're not an employee but have income from self employment? You may be able to establish a plan for yourself. Say you're age 60, serve on the board of a couple of corporations, earning $250,000 annually in director's fees. You may be able to establish a defined benefit pension plan and contribute and deduct about $130,000 annually until you must begin minimum required distributions by April 1st of the year following that in which you turn 70½. Your first year's distribution (assuming your spouse is not more than 10 years younger, or you're single) would only be 1/27.4 of your accumulated plan balance. While subsequent years' distributions increase annually, significant income tax deferral is achieved. Undistributed funds could be bequeathed to a child who could spread distributions over her lifetime. Alternatively, a bequest to your private foundation or other charity would be income and estate tax free. Be aware that if you have employees, they generally must be included in the plan.

Individual Retirement Accounts

Due to their modest contribution limit of $6000 ($7000 if you're age 50 or older) adjusted for inflation, a "contributory" IRA may be of limited benefit. But contributions are deductible (assuming you aren't covered by a company retirement plan) and investment earnings grow tax deferred until withdrawn at age 70½. As with a qualified plan, described above, your first year's distribution would only be 1/27.4 of your accumulation balance. While subsequent years' distributions increase annually, income deferral results.

There is, however, another use for an IRA. You can roll over some or all of the balance of your profit sharing or pension plan into a "self-directed"

IRA when you cease participation, for example upon retirement or sale of your business. Profit sharing plans, in particular, can permit "in service" distributions for those who qualify, allowing you to continue plan participation. In lieu of investing in traditional assets such as mutual funds, publicly traded stocks or bonds, you could invest in real estate or a private business venture, achieving the same benefits of tax deferral and protection from external creditors. But care must be taken to ensure you do not engage in a prohibited transaction between yourself and your IRA, which include the following:

– buying, exchanging, or renting property
– lending to or borrowing from (including a loan guarantee to)
– personal use of goods, services or facilities
– deriving direct or indirect benefit such as providing seed capital for your son's business or an employment opportunity for your daughter.

Also, an IRA investing in an active trade or business would be taxed on its unrelated business taxable income (UBTI). In contrast, investing in a partnership which owns an apartment complex generally would not.

A word about asset location. While offering the advantage of tax deferral, distributions from IRA's, 401K's, defined benefit, and other retirement accounts are generally treated as ordinary income. This includes income otherwise taxed as long-term capital gains and dividends, which normally receive preferential tax treatment (i.e., currently a maximum of 23.8% at the federal level, including the 3.8% Affordable Care Act tax on investment income). In a sense, this income is converted to a form taxed less favorably. Therefore, it is generally advisable, to the extent practical, to invest in growth-oriented assets generating capital gains or tax-sheltered income (e.g., stocks and stock mutual funds and real estate) in a taxable portfolio and bonds and other investments generating ordinary income in tax deferred accounts (guided, of course, by your overall asset allocation).

C Corporation/January 31st Fiscal Year

A business can be structured as a C corporation, and obtain the advantages of electing a fiscal year and utilizing potentially lower corporate tax brackets. As previously discussed, the Tax Cuts and Jobs Act of 2017 reduced the top rate applicable to C corporations from 35 to 21%. In addition to accumulation of earnings taxed at lower rates (subject to limitations on accumulation of earnings), tax deferral can be obtained through selection of a January 31st fiscal year. This permits the corporation to accrue earnings until the final month of its tax year, pay them in January to the individual or his pass-through entity which receives the benefit of the income soon after the close of his personal tax year, but with liability for tax payment not occurring potentially until April 15th of the following year (subject to rules for minimum withholding). Hence a one-year tax deferral is obtained, which has growing value in corporations with increasing earnings. Under certain circumstances it may be advantageous to distribute accumulated income as a dividend. And upon liquidation, 100% of the gain may be excluded (up to $10 million) if the company qualifies as a Qualified Small Business Corporation. This provision is discussed later in this chapter.

Salary and Bonus Deferral

Related to the concept of business income deferral is salary deferral, applicable if you are a senior executive of a major corporation. Deferring a portion of your salary or a bonus allows you to defer paying income taxes on it until the future date at which it is received. Assuming the deferred income earns a return comparable to what you could have obtained, deferring income can work to your advantage, especially if when ultimately received you will be in a lower tax bracket. The corporation will pay tax on the deferred income, but receives a deduction when the deferred income is paid out. Deferring compensation has gained additional appeal after the Tax Cuts and Jobs Act of 2017 due to the reduction of the top rate for C corporations to 21% from 35% (and unlike for provisions relating to personal income taxation, the corporate tax cut isn't subject to the 2025 "sunset" provision).

A formal non-qualified deferred compensation plan may be offered to a select group of highly compensated executives. These plans can be quite flexible, with no government-imposed limits on the amount of employee deferral, or employer contribution, in contrast to qualified plans. But unlike qualified retirement plans, monies must be subject to the company's creditors and funds may not be formally earmarked to secure your future benefits. Further, social security tax will still apply to deferrals (though benefits will not be taxed).

Investment Income

Charitable Remainder Trust

Discussed in Chapter 3, Charitable Planning, a Charitable Remainder Trust (CRT) allows you to defer and potentially eliminate altogether gain recognition upon sale of an appreciated asset. As typically designed, the trust will pay you and your spouse, if applicable, income for your lifetime with the remaining principal paid to the charity of your choosing, including a private foundation. As the trust is tax exempt, it pays no income tax on the sale of the appreciated asset. Rather, gain is only taxable to you to the extent it is distributed, based upon a "tiered" approach as discussed earlier. So if distributions do not exceed ordinary income, capital gains are deferred.

Deferred Annuity

Contributions are generally made after tax, but investment earnings grow tax deferred until withdrawn. Another tax advantage is that upon annuitization (i.e., where the insurance company guarantees a lifetime income stream), a portion of each payment is characterized as a return of your original investment and therefore tax-free.

Annuity products come in two varieties: fixed (including fixed-indexed) and variable. Traditional fixed annuities provide a bond-like return. Fixed-indexed annuities provide a crediting rate linked to an index, such as the S&P 500, but often with a floor or guaranteed minimum return. Variable annuities allow you to select from numerous sub accounts managed by leading mutual fund companies, representing many asset classes. Unlike IRAs and other qualified plans, there is no legal restriction on the amount of your earnings, your annual contributions or ultimate accumulation. Hence they offer flexibility other savings arrangements may not. Other features such as income guarantees and death benefits may be added, at an additional cost. Annuity products entail expenses and surrender charges which must be considered as well.

Employee Stock Ownership Plan

If you are contemplating the sale of your business, one option is to sell to your employees through an Employee Stock Ownership Plan or ESOP. As discussed in Chapter 4, Business Succession Planning, you can sell your stock to the ESOP and recognize no gain as long as your purchase quali-fied replacement securities no earlier than three months before and up to 12 months after. Such securities must be publicly traded common stock or corporate bonds, the most popular being long-dated (i.e., 50-year maturity) corporate bonds. If held until your death, the securities will receive a step up in basis to the then fair market value, eliminating the gain.

Health Savings Account (HSA)

Individuals covered by a high deductible health plan are eligible to make pre-tax/tax deductible contributions to an HSA of up to $3500 if single or $7000 for a family ($4500 or $8000 if you're age 50 or older), adjusted for inflation. There is no earnings restriction. Withdrawals for qualified medical expenses are tax free. Since unused funds continue to grow on a tax-deferred basis, this presents a tax planning opportunity by paying non-insured medical expenses out-of-pocket and allowing HSA funds to accumulate. While contributions are no longer allowed once you're Medicare-eligible at age 65, health care distributions continue to be tax free. Other distributions are taxed as ordinary income but are penalty tax free if taken after age 65. And unlike with a traditional IRA or retirement plan, there are no mini-mum required distributions.

Installment Sale

Another tax deferral strategy is an installment sale, such as of real estate or a business, and is a disposition in which at least one payment is to be received after the close of the tax year of disposition. Sellers eligible to use the installment method of reporting (i.e., you cannot be deemed a "dealer" selling from your inventory) can defer tax on the sale and have gain recog-nized in proportion to the installment payments received. An installment sale should be supported by a written promissory note obligating the buyer to make at least one payment in the year of sale. Each payment received is divided among the return of basis, profit on the sale, and interest income. Depreciation recapture income is fully recognized in the year of an install-ment sale of depreciable property, even if no principal payments are received in that year. If you have the option to receive full price upon sale, you should weigh the economic risk of deferred payments against the tax savings. Installment sale treatment is automatic unless you opt to recognize the gain fully in the year of disposition.

Private Placement Life Insurance

This is a specialized form of life insurance offered only to accredited investors or qualified purchasers (i.e., who satisfy minimum income, net worth or other requirements). As discussed in Chapter 6, life insurance enjoys specific tax benefits including income-tax-deferred growth of cash value, tax-free withdrawals if taken as loans, and a tax-free death benefit. If owned in an irrevocable trust, the death benefit will also pass estate tax-free. The product is designed to take advantage of those benefits to enhance the after-tax return of otherwise tax-inefficient investments (such as hedge funds, often taxed at ordinary income rates). The policy must be funded with cash, not individual investments, and often entails annual premiums of $1 million or more, paid over a four or five year period. Essentially a specialized form of variable universal life insurance, but in lieu of the customary mutual fund like sub-accounts they offer, the investment options are referred to as Insurance Dedicated Funds, typically hedge fund-like vehicles. Investments can be added to an insurance company's offering at the owner's request, with manager and fund changes made without triggering recognition of gain. However the policy owner cannot exercise such discretion as to be deemed to be the owner of the underlying fund assets.

Qualified Opportunity Zone

A provision of the Tax Cuts and Jobs Act of 2017, a Qualified Opportunity Zone is an economically-distressed area in which a new investment may receive tax-preferred treatment. Investors may defer prior investment gains (e.g., from securities or real estate) if the gains are invested into a Qualified Opportunity Fund (QOF) within 180 days of the gain-triggering event (i.e., sale or exchange). Deferral continues until the earlier of the date on which the investment in a QOF is sold or exchanged, or December 31, 2026. Additionally, if a taxpayer holds the QOF investment at least five years, the taxpayer may exclude 10% of the original deferred gain. For a seven year holding period, the exclusion is 15%. If the taxpayer holds the investment in the QOF for at least 10 years, the taxpayer may elect to increase the basis of the QOF investment equal to its fair market value on the date that the QOF investment is sold or exchanged. This may eliminate all or a substantial amount of gain due to appreciation on the QOF investment. Obviously, an investment in an Opportunity Zone involves considerable risk which must be carefully considered, the tax benefits notwithstanding.

Qualified Small Business Stock

Section 1045 of the Internal Revenue Code allows for the deferral of gain on the sale of a business which you have held for at least six months and which meets the following criteria:

- A U.S. "C" corporation from inception, having issued its stock after August 10, 1993
- Purchased upon original issuance
- Having less than $50 million in gross assets at the time of issuance
- At least 80% of assets used in active conduct of one or more qualified trade or businesses. Generally excluded are professional services (e.g., law, medicine, accounting), financial services (e.g., banking, insurance, finance), restaurants and lodging, and mining and oil and gas production.

Proceeds of sale must be re-invested into a new qualifying business within 60 days of the sale of the existing company.

The stock may be personally owned, or owned indirectly through a partnership, limited liability company or "S" corporation. Of course numerous other technical requirements apply.

Another tax relief provision relating to the sale of a business resides in Section 1202 of the Code. Mentioned earlier under C Corporation/Fiscal Year, it allows for the exemption of between 50 and 100% (depending upon year of issuance—100% if after September 27, 2010) of gain up to the greater of $10 million or 10 times the taxpayer's basis. Qualification requirements are similar to those for Section 1045 above with a notable exception that the holding period is five years. Also, the tax rate applicable to the taxable portion of the gain is 28% compared to the current maximum rate of 20%. This notwithstanding, Section 1202 can still yield an advantage.

Tax Deferred Exchange

If you own investment real estate and are desirous of selling, you might want to consider a 1031 tax-free exchange. Property held for investment can be traded for other like-kind investment property without incurring tax liability. The potential tax on the gain is postponed to a time when the exchanged property is sold at a price exceeding the tax basis of the property. A potential tax due on gain from depreciation recapture may also be deferred. To qualify as a tax-free exchange of real estate, the transaction must have the following key elements: the property is held for productive use in trade or business, or for investment; there must be an exchange—a reciprocal transfer of value; property exchange must be of like-kind. If the like-kind exchange requires the payment or receipt of money to equalize the values of the properties that are being exchanged, the exchange of money or other property not qualifying as like-kind property will be treated as taxable to the recipient. This property is known as "boot." When mortgaged property is transferred by a taxpayer in an exchange, the mortgage is included in the amount realized on transfer. However, gain is only recognized to the extent of boot. Real property (for example a building) cannot be exchanged for personal property (a partnership investing in real estate) and have the exchange classified as a like-kind tax-free exchange.

Tax Free Reorganization

More appropriately considered a tax deferral strategy, this applies when one corporation acquires another. Considered an "acquisitive reorganization" under Section 368 of the Internal Revenue Code, the transaction may be structured as either an asset deal—the purchase of the selling company's assets, or a stock acquisition. The result is that the owner of the selling/target corporation acquires stock in the acquiring or parent company with the same tax basis. Gain may ultimately be recognized upon sale of the acquiring company's stock.

Tax Loss Harvesting

If you own stocks, bonds, mutual funds, or exchange-traded funds (ETFs) in which you have losses, and they are held in a taxable account, this idea may be for you. You can "harvest" the loss by selling the security, and replacing it with a similar investment. For example, you could sell a bond trading at a discount from par value, then replace it with one trading at a similar discount, which upon redemption, will result in recovering your original investment.

Losses first offset capital gains; the excess, if any of capital losses over capital gains, is deductible from ordinary income to the extent of $3000. Losses on the sale of stock or securities are not deductible if, with a period beginning 30 days before the date of the sale and ending 30 days after the date of the sale, substantially identical securities are acquired. This is the so-called "wash rule."

Conversion

Corporate Loans to Shareholders/Employees

In the context of a C corporation, a loan may be taken in lieu of salary, hence avoiding income and payroll taxes thereon. The loan must be properly documented, and require periodic payments of principal and interest at the government prescribed rate, in order to avoid characterization as a constructive dividend. This strategy is not available to an employee of a publicly-listed corporation.

Death

Death is the "Holy Grail" of tax planning for appreciated assets. Given its inevitability, the income tax and wealth transfer opportunities require careful consideration. Most assets receive a basis adjustment to fair market value at the owner's death (notably excepted are retirement accounts such as profit sharing and pension plans, along with certain other assets). This basis "step up" eliminates gain in appreciated assets (including "negative basis" in investment partnerships), allowing for tax-free sale or a new basis for depreciation in depreciable assets.

Gift and sale strategies, such as those discussed in Chapter 2, generally seek to shift the growth of appreciating assets to the next generation(s), eliminating future estate tax liability in the donor's estate. However, the estate tax savings must be compared to the income tax benefit of the basis step up, especially with an older donor or individual with a shortened life expectancy due to poor health. As discussed in Chapter 2, a strategy for situations where assets were previously transferred (e.g., to an intentionally defective grantor trust) is for the donor to exchange or purchase the asset for cash, returning it to his/her estate (while having shifted the appreciation). If there is insufficient cash, the donor could borrow from a commercial lender, secured by other assets or perhaps the asset to be purchased.

Educational Savings Account

Often referred to as a 529 plan (named after the IRS Code Section that authorizes it), investment gains are tax free if used for "qualified expenses," including tuition, fees, books, room and board, and certain other expenses at an eligible education institution (e.g., college or graduate school, post-secondary vocational or trade school). And up to $10,000 annually may be used for tuition for elementary and secondary schools. If the monies are not fully used by one beneficiary, a new beneficiary who is a member of the family of the original beneficiary may be substituted. Non-qualifying distributions will be subject to ordinary income tax plus a 10% penalty.

The maximum annual contribution (without incurring a gift tax) is currently $15,000. This amount is doubled if both parents open accounts for each beneficiary (or for that matter if grandma and grandpa fund accounts for their grandchildren). A contributor may make a gift of up to $75,000 per beneficiary in one year without triggering federal gift tax (treated as if spread over a five-year period). The total accumulation in any account varies by state but may be up to $500,000 or more. Other differences may exist, for example California does not currently allow tax free distributions for elementary and secondary school expenses.

Municipal Bonds

An income-converting strategy is investing in tax-exempt municipal bonds instead of taxable corporate or U.S. government bonds. The nominal (i.e., money equivalent) yield on a municipal bond is less than the yield on a taxable bond of comparable maturity and quality. But the taxable equivalent yield (found by dividing the tax-free municipal bond yield by one minus your effective tax bracket both state and federal if the bond is issued by the state in which you reside), is generally higher than the corporate or U.S. bond. So this strategy is generally advantageous for high bracket taxpayers. Municipal bonds come in many forms: general obligation, utility, school and hospital, each with different risk, return, and liquidity characteristics which should be considered.

Variable Rate Demand Notes (VRDNs) are long term municipal securities converted into a money market instrument by their daily or weekly put feature. They often are backed by a letter of credit, strengthening their credit standing. VRDNs are the principal holding in tax exempt money market funds but investors with, generally, $3 million or greater to invest may have a custom portfolio of these securities which are generally issued in $100,000 denominations.

New State of Residence

While income tax planning is principally focused on the Federal Income Tax, state income taxation can be a significant factor as well. California's is the highest with a top rate of 13.3%. But others aren't far behind; residents of New York City pay a combined 12.7% state and city income tax. But seven states have no income tax at all: Alaska, Florida, Nevada, South Dakota, Washington, Wyoming, and Texas. So changing your state of residence may be a viable strategy, especially if you aren't tied to a business that you're unwilling to relocate. Indeed this strategy may have acquired increased appeal after the Tax Cuts and Jobs Act of 2017, which limits the federal deduction for state and local tax to just $10,000, increasing their effective cost.

Generally five factors are considered in determining if you have changed your domicile for tax purposes. They include: physical presence (generally at least 183 days), home, family, and business activities (a home office in your new residence probably won't suffice), personal property and documentary evidence (e.g., driver's license, voter registration, banking relationships, church/synagogue/mosque and country club affiliation, doctors, etc.). Regardless, the state in which your business and real properties are physically located will continue to levy its tax.

Rent in Lieu of Salary

If you are a business owner, you could personally acquire equipment or real estate used in the business. It could then be leased back to the business utilizing an "arms length" lease agreement, including market rate rents. Income tax deductions normally available to property owners, such as depreciation, interest, taxes, insurance and maintenance are fully deductible to the extent of rental income. Excess income would be eligible for sheltering from any other passive activities; excess deductions could shelter passive income from other activities.

Roth IRA

While the contribution must be made with after-tax earnings, if held for at least five years, your investment gains will be tax free upon distribution. Had you invested those monies traditionally, they would have been taxed annually. Unfortunately, contribution limits are modest (only $6000, $7000 if age 50 or older—inflation adjusted), and income eligibility is low ($137,000 single taxpayer, $203,000 joint, inflation adjusted). So while not a practical opportunity for you, it may be for your children or grandchildren. For example, they could make a contribution from their earned income, facilitated by a tax free gift from you utilizing your $15,000 annual exclusion.

Given the relative attractiveness of Roth IRA tax treatment and exemption from age 70½ minimum required distribution rules, traditional IRA conversion and retirement plan rollovers to a Roth IRA are worth considering. The implications of a Roth IRA conversion or retirement plan rollover are as follows. First and foremost, funds rolled over must be reported as ordinary income in the year of conversion if they were pre-tax contributions (i.e., a retirement plan rollover or deductible IRA). So rather than deferring the tax, you are accelerating it in the interest of later enjoying tax free income. And, importantly, there is no income stipulation to qualify to do a conversion (giving rise to the label "back door" Roth).

Following are factors that generally *favor* a Roth conversion:

- you expect to be in a comparable or higher tax bracket in your retirement years
- you have monies outside the accounts you are converting with which to pay the tax (the analysis is seldom favorable if the converted funds must themselves be used to pay the tax)
- you have a tax loss or tax credit that could be used to mitigate the tax burden
- you will not necessarily need all the funds during your retirement and desire to leave an income tax-free asset to your heirs (remember that Roth IRAs are exempt from minimum required distributions by the account owner, though beneficiaries must distribute over their lifetime).

If you are not yet age 59½, distributions taken within five years of conversion are generally subject to a 10% penalty, except for limited exceptions including distributions taken as substantially equal periodic payments. A final thought: you may do a partial conversion over a period of years in order to spread out the tax hit.

Diverting

Gifts to Children

A strategy for diverting income entails gifts of income-producing property or cash to family members that are taxed at a lower rate. You may be able to reduce your family's overall tax burden by shifting some income to children in lower tax brackets. For example, you might consider transferring selected investments to your dependent children. Beware, however, the "Kiddie Tax." For dependent children under the age of 18 (under age 24 if a full-time student whose earned income does not exceed half of his or her own support for the year) the first $2100 of investment income will be tax free. Ordinary income above this threshold is taxed at the compressed tax brackets of estates and trusts, from 10 to 37%. The first $2600 of dividends and capital gains are eligible for the zero capital gain rate with amounts in excess taxed at 15% or 20%. Once a child reaches age 18 (or 24), the Kiddie Tax no longer applies. To avoid the Kiddie Tax, you may wish to consider allocating your children's assets to investments producing little current taxable income (e.g., such as growth stock mutual funds which pay a modest dividend).

Pass-Through Distributions in Lieu of a Salary

If you're the sole owner of a business structured as a pass-through entity (e.g., Sub-S, LLC or partnerships), you may be able to reduce your salary, distributing the difference as profits. This could yield a savings in social security and Medicare as well as federal and state unemployment taxes. The IRS is, of course, on to this strategy and substantial penalties apply to underpayment of payroll taxes. Hence it is important to ensure that reasonable compensation is paid, along with corresponding payroll taxes. Of course, if the company has multiple owners, forgone salary (and that of other owners) will be distributed with a possible dilutive result.

Deductions

Under the Tax Cuts and Jobs Act of 2017 (effective 2018–2025, unless extended), itemized deductions were curtailed; deductions for state and local taxes are limited to $10,000, deduction for home mortgage interest is generally limited to a $750,000 mortgage, and miscellaneous itemized deductions were eliminated. Fortunately, certain deductions remain.

Bunching deductions for medical expenses, to the extent feasible, will facilitate exceeding the 7.5% of AGI threshold for deductibility.

It is also possible to create deductions through certain investments. The prime example is investment in real estate, which was discussed in Chapter 7: Investment Management. You can take deductions for operating expenses, mortgage interest and depreciation which, if they exceed your income, may be deductible against other income up to $25,000 (assuming your adjusted gross income does not exceed $150,000 annually), or without limit against other "passive" income.

An investment in an oil and gas program may represent another opportunity for accredited investors. Structured as non-traded partnerships, they typically involve "developmental" drilling—new wells in proven oil fields. Tax benefits include an 80–90% first year deduction owing to intangible drilling costs and cash distributions sheltered by the oil and gas depletion allowance.

Charitable Contributions

Another deduction yielding strategy is to make contributions to a charity either in property or cash. A cash contribution to "public" organizations (for example, education and medical institutions, churches and publicly supported charitable organizations) is currently deductible up to 60% of adjusted gross income up to the amount of the gift (under the Tax Cuts and Jobs Act, the amount reverts to its prior 50% level in 2026). Contributions to organizations other than those mentioned above are generally limited to 30%. Amounts not deductible in the current year are permitted a five-year carry forward.

Charitable contributions of an appreciated asset wherein all or a portion of the gain would be capital gain result in a deduction of 30% of adjusted gross income (if made to a public charity) or 20% if made to other than a public charity. If you're contemplating a charitable gift and have appreciated securities, donating them is a smart move as both you and the charity pay no tax on the gain.

Cost Segregation

Cost segregation may be a useful strategy for accelerating deductions. Residential property and commercial property is generally depreciable over 27.5 years and 39 years, respectively. Yet certain building improvements may be eligible for depreciation over 5, 7 or 15-year periods. Examples include electrical systems, mechanical components, plumbing and finishes. An "engineering-based" cost segregation study must be obtained to support this approach.

Home Mortgage Interest

Home mortgage interest is currently deductible on balances of up to $750,000 ($1 million if in place before the effective date of the Tax Cuts and Jobs Act of 2017). Many wealthy individuals maintain balances far in excess of the deductible amount, while others prefer to own their home mortgage free. From an economic standpoint, one should carry the maximum balance for which interest is deductible. Home mortgage interest is some of the cheapest financing available. So the after-tax cost is almost always less than the after-tax return on an acceptable investment purchased with funds otherwise used to pay off the mortgage.

Incomplete Non-grantor Trust

As discussed in Chapter 2, trusts offer substantial estate planning benefits, especially those where the grantor pays the trust's income tax (i.e., a defective grantor trust). Under the Tax Cuts and Jobs Act of 2017, non-grantor trusts have garnered increased interest by, for example, facilitating the deduction of state and local income taxes otherwise limited to $10,000.

The strategy entails the creation of a trust in one of several states with no income tax and which allows self-settled trusts (discussed in Chapter 4). The latter feature allows the trustor to be a beneficiary of the trust, along with, for example, his or her children and grandchildren, as long as distributions to the grantor are made with the consent of a distribution committee consisting of the other beneficiaries. The trust could be a means to capture the temporary increase in the transfer tax exemption before its expiration or could be structured to be "incomplete" for transfer tax purposes (remaining in the taxable estate) if the exemptions were fully allocated elsewhere.

As an example, an individual who owns a primary or secondary residence with property taxes of $40,000 ($30,000 above the deduction limit) could transfer a one quarter interest to four trusts of which the grantor and his or her spouse, along with a different child for each, are beneficiaries. In addition, assets with income sufficient to pay the property tax would also be contributed. As each trust would be eligible for its own $10,000 deduction, the result would be fully deductible of the property tax in addition to freeing up the grantor's $10,000 limit for other state or local income tax deductions. The grantors could continue to reside in the residence with no income or gift tax implications.

As with any strategy, there are a number of considerations, not the least of which include the gift of one's home; others include potential property re-assessment and loan restrictions. Additionally, the IRS may seek to collapse the individual trusts into one, with resulting loss of property tax deductions.

AMT

No discussion of income taxes would be complete without mention of the alternative minimum tax or AMT, for short. The AMT is the government's attempt to curtail too much of a good thing by insuring that there is a minimum tax that taxpayers with numerous deductions and other tax preferences pay. While as a result of the Tax Cuts and Jobs Act of 2017, the reach of the AMT should be significantly curtailed for 2018 through 2025, it is still a relevant consideration for many wealthy tax payers.

The AMT formula is essentially as follows: start with your taxable income, then add back certain deductions (i.e. those disallowed under the AMT), add in tax preference items (i.e. tax breaks such as for Qualified Small Business Stock, discussed earlier), subtract the AMT exemption then multiply the result by the AMT tax rate of 26% or 28%. The excess of the AMT over your regular income tax is added to the latter to yield your tax liability. Planning to mitigate the impact of the AMT is a tricky undertaking and usually requires planning over multiple consecutive years.

Stock Options: The Risks and Rewards

If you're a corporate executive, chances are you participate in a stock option plan. While these plans represent an attractive fringe benefit, extracting maximum value from them can be a challenging task. Stock options basically come in two forms: Incentive Stock Options (ISOs) and regular or Non-qualified Options (Non-Quals). The two important questions, regardless of the type of option you have, are: when to exercise them and, secondly, when to sell the stock after you've acquired it through exercise.

Let's address the exercise question first. As a rule of thumb, its best to exercise options as late as possible before option expiration. This allows you to maximize the leverage inherent in the option. One constraint with ISO's, however, is that sale cannot be earlier than one year after exercise and two years after grant (Note, however, that if you are in an AMT situation, a disqualifying sale may be a useful tactic).

Here's a quick list of strategies for disposing of it. The most straightforward is to simply sell your shares and pay your tax. With a top federal rate of 23.8% plus any state income tax, you'll probably keep 70 cents on the dollar. To avoid insider-trading problems, consider filing a "10b 5-1" plan with the SEC, evidencing a pre-arrangement to dispose of your stock. This will facilitate disciplined diversification through an advanced commitment.

You should also consider gifts of stock to your children, allowing them to recognize gain in their potentially lower bracket. Or you may wish to consider gifts to charity. If a charitable remainder trust is the beneficiary, you'll benefit from the income from the portfolio created with the sale proceeds of your gifted stock. Still another strategy involves taking a margin loan against your company stock and using the proceeds to build your diversified portfolio. You can initially borrow up to 50% of the value of most stock. Even with the leverage of your margin loan, your overall portfolio risk could be lower. You could also consider protecting against a decline in the price of the stock by establishing a colar: purchasing put (option to sell) options and selling call (option to buy) options on the stock.

Questions to Consider

* Have you or your tax advisor considered available tax planning strategies in the context of "defer, convert, divert, deduct"?
* Have you considered the impact of the Tax Cuts and Jobs Act of 2017? Does the 21% rate applicable to C corporations present a planning opportunity?
* If you live in a high-income tax state, have you considered strategies specifically designed to reduce the additional burden?

9

Selecting a Financial Planner

Let men be wise by instinct if they can, but when this fails be wise by good advice.

—Sophocles, Greek playwright

In the last eight chapters we have covered topics ranging from the efficient frontier to charitable lead trusts and from private placement life insurance to wait and see buy-sell agreements. Each of these concepts, along with the others discussed, is, most likely, familiar to an individual currently on your advisory team: your CPA, attorney, stockbroker or others. Yet, how often were you left less than confident that the concepts presented had been adequately vetted by your advisors as to their applicability to you? Have they been appropriately integrated into a comprehensive plan that continues to evolve with your situation and needs?

If you are like most wealthy individuals, you consult with your advisors as frequently as a need presents itself: to file your taxes, advise on a business transaction, or make an investment. Each area of your planning, most likely, has been structured at different times, with different advisors, each with their own perspective. Besides, you're busy and it's difficult to find the time to bring all of your advisors together in the same room to discuss the "big picture," not to mention coordinating the activities that must follow.

This is where a financial planner can help. He'll work with you, your spouse and children, as necessary, to understand and help you crystallize and articulate your objectives. He'll assess your current arrangements in the context of your objectives, identifying inconsistencies, gaps, and shortcomings. He'll explore with you alternatives and new strategies you hadn't considered.

© The Author(s) 2019
R. P. Rojeck, *Wealth*,
https://doi.org/10.1007/978-3-030-24497-2_9

He'll help bring your existing advisors into the process and perhaps intro-
duce others to you as well (e.g., an expert on structuring charitable gifts
or a family business consultant). Finally, after the plan is agreed upon and
reduced to writing, he will assist you in its implementation. Some have
described the financial planner's role as the "quarterback" of the advisory
team. However you define it, the greater your wealth and more complex
your affairs, the more you cannot afford to do without it.

Choose Wisely

Choosing a financial planner is a project all its own, because they are not all
created equal. In general, however, they will be subject to regulation by both
the federal and state governments. The Securities Exchange Commission
(SEC) regulates financial planners as to their investment advisory activities,
such as when they are providing financial advice or managing money for
a fee. The Financial Industry Regulatory Authority (FINRA) regulates
financial planners as to the sale of securities (for example mutual funds,
bonds, and limited partnerships) as a registered representative of a broker
dealer. The states regulate financial planner activities relating to the sale of
insurance products and in some cases investment advisory activities.

In choosing a financial planner, I suggest you focus on the following seven
criteria:

- Professional credential
- Years of experience
- Educational background
- Specialization
- Disciplinary proceedings
- Firm affiliation
- References

Let's take a brief look at each.

Credential

Just as you would expect a doctor, dentist, lawyer or accountant to have
a credential, it is no less applicable for a financial planner. A variety of
credentials may be held by financial planners today. Some are specific to

the financial planning discipline while others represent expertise in one of its components, such as investments, for example. I will focus here on the top three financial planning designations. The best known is the Certified Financial Planner or CFP® designation. The requirements for attainment of the CFP® designation currently are as follows:

* Have at least a bachelor's level degree
* Complete the CFP® course of education at a CFP Board-registered institution
* Pass a six-hour comprehensive exam
* Have three years of qualified full-time work experience (two years if under the direct supervision of a CFP® professional and engaged in delivery of personal financial planning for clients)
* Pass a background check and agree to adhere to a code of ethics
* Complete 30 hours of continuing education, bi-annually, after licensing

The CFP Board of Standards is the regulatory body for CFPs and approves programs at colleges and universities that offer the financial planning curriculum. It also maintains a registry of its licensees, which can be accessed through the following:

* Website: www.cfp.net
* Phone: 888-237-6275

The primary membership association for Certified Financial Planners is the Financial Planning Association (FPA). Financial planner members must be CFP® professionals. You may access this planner member list by contacting the following:

* Website: www.fpanet.org
* Phone: 800-322-4237

The second credential is Chartered Financial Consultant (ChFC). The requirements for the acquisition and maintenance of the ChFC credential are as follows:

* Complete the ChFC course of education offered through the American College
* Have three years of qualified full-time work experience
* Adhere to a code of ethics

- Complete 30 hours of continuing education, bi-annually, after credentialing.

If you are interested in locating a ChFC you can do so by contacting the American College at the following:

- Website: www.theamericancollege.edu
- Phone: 1-888-263-7265

The primary membership organization for ChFC's is the Society of Financial Services Professionals. They maintain a referral program and can be reached at:

- Website: www.financialpro.org
- Phone: 610-526-2500

The third of the leading credentials is Personal Financial Specialist. This credential is held only by Certified Public Accountants so you will normally see CPA-PFS. States regulate the practice of accounting and the licensing of CPAs, so you can find them through your state board of accountancy. In order to obtain the PFS credential, the individual must complete an exam and is subject to recertification every three years.

The primary membership association for the CPA-FPS is the American Institute of Certified Public Accountants. You can access a list of those holding a CPA-PFS credential on the AICPA website at:

- Website: www.aicpa.org
- Phone: 212-596-6200 or 888-777-7077.

Experience

There is no absolute standard here. Just use your judgment. This is no different than evaluating any other professional: generally the more experience the better. However, you may feel most comfortable with a planner of a certain age, which may suggest a certain level of experience.

Educational Background

In addition to a professional credential, you should inquire about the prospective advisor's academic background. While I consider this secondary to a professional credential, and the CFP® designation and CPA-PFS credentials require at least a bachelor's degree, it is nonetheless relevant. Degrees to look for would be bachelor's degree, master's degree or even Ph.D. Of course, it would be beneficial if the degree was in a related field such as business or finance.

Specialization

Again, just as in other professions, financial planners will tend to work in a certain area and consequently develop expertise in it. Examples include: business owners, real estate developers, or corporate executives. Others may also have a specialty in investment management or insurance. All things considered, it is better to work with a planner with experience unique to your situation.

Disciplinary Actions

Yet another factor in choosing a financial planner is whether he or she has had any prior or currently pending disciplinary actions imposed by either the credentialing or governmental regulatory body. This information can be obtained from the website or by calling the regulatory body. They are listed below:

* The Financial Industry Regulatory Authority (FINRA) website: www. finra.org; phone: 800-289-9999
* The Securities Exchange Commission (SEC) website: http://www.sec.gov; phone: 240-386-4848
* State Insurance Department's websites vary but you can generally contact them through the National Association of Insurance Commissioners (NAIC) website at http://www.naic.org/state_web_map.htm. Or you can call 816-842-3600.

The Code of Ethics of each of the three credentialing bodies requires that the planner inform the body of any pending disciplinary action by any regulatory body. Violation of applicable securities or insurance regulations may, depending upon the circumstances, result in loss of credential. These bodies may post disciplinary actions on their websites as well.

Affiliation

Again, there is no right or wrong answer to this question. A financial planner may own his own firm or be a member of a small group practice or be with a large national firm. The relevance of the size of firm basically is two-fold: continuity and resources. If the planner is a solo practitioner, a relevant question would be, "what happens if something happens to you?" In the event of the death, disability or retirement of your advisor, is there someone who will continue service with minimal disruption? In a larger firm, it is more likely, though not automatic, that service continuity will occur.

Compensation

The method of compensation was not listed as one of the seven criteria, as I do not believe it is a factor in determining the quality of advice or reliability of service. The method of compensation is not good or bad but you should be clear about it going into a relationship with your advisor. There are three basic methods of compensation used by financial planners with some variations as well. The following is a brief discussion of each.

"**Fee Only**"—Advisors compensated in this fashion charge a fee for planning advice and if they offer investment management services will do so for a fee. They do not receive commissions resulting from the sale of securities or insurance products. Consequently, they will generally refer those transactions, notably insurance, to other advisors. Incidentally, there is a membership organization for fee-only advisors known as the National Association of Personal Financial Advisors (NAPFA). If you are interested in knowing more, their website is www.napfa.org or you can contact them at 847-483-5400 ext. 100 or 847-483-5400 ext. 106.

"**Commission and Fee**"—Also referred to as fee-based, these advisors will generally charge a fee for planning advice, and if they offer investment management services will generally do so for a fee. If this is the scope of the services your advisor is doing, there is little practical distinction between a "fee only" and "fee based" advisor. However, the latter may also offer products for which they receive a commission. Insurance products such as annuities as well as disability, long-term care and life insurance are examples.

"**Commission**"—In this form of compensation, the advisor's compensation is predicated upon your purchase of investment or insurance products from her. The advisor may still offer planning advice as a part of their relationship with you to facilitate the proper fit of the products being recommended.

References

Once you have pretty well decided on your new advisor, before giving him or her the go ahead, be sure to ask for and speak with references from their other clients.

Fiduciary Status

A term frequently used in the context of advice is *fiduciary*, generally defined as one who acts on behalf of another and assumes a duty to act in good faith and with care and loyalty in fulfilling the obligation. Individuals regulated by the Securities Exchange Commission as Registered Investment Advisors are held to a fiduciary standard when providing investment or financial planning advice. Individuals rendering advice to retirement plans are also considered fiduciaries. In contrast, advisors acting in the capacity of a securities broker, regulated by FINRA, or an insurance agent, regulated under state law, are not so obliged, but nonetheless must adhere to established standards. Those holding the CFP® designation or CPA-PFS designations must adhere to a fiduciary standard as stipulated by their certifying body.

What to Expect

Once you have decided upon the right planner for you, if that planner is following the process prescribed by the CFP Board of Standards, you can expect him or her to employ the following six-step process:

* Discuss with you the scope of the services to be provided, each party's responsibilities, the process and likely time frame involved, her method of compensation and any conflicts of interest.
* Gather information about your personal and financial goals and other relevant information. Learn about your current arrangements and collect financial documents as necessary.
* Analyze the information and evaluate to what extent your goals can be met by your existing resources and current course of action.
* Develop and present recommendations tailored to your situation.
* Work with you and other advisors to implement your plan.
* Meet with you periodically (usually at least annually) to monitor progress and modify or update your plan as necessary.

The Team

In the Preface I described what I see as a commonplace issue for wealthy individuals—a lack of coordination in their financial arrangements. And throughout I have described the role a financial planner can play in helping address this issue. Your current advisory team no doubt consists of estate and business attorneys and perhaps other legal area specialists. It includes your accountant(s) and experts in investments and insurance as well. But a key member, often considered the quarterback of the team, is the financial planner, someone who will take the "30,000 foot view," then drill down on specific issues, coordinating the activities of others, to produce a comprehensive plan. And a financial planner can help ensure the plan remains up to date throughout the years. Hopefully this chapter will aid you in selecting the right one for you.

10

Tying It All Together

We have covered a lot of ground since we began our journey nine chapters ago. For those who have made the journey with me, I offer my congratulations on your fortitude and perseverance.

It's often said that it's easier to make money than to keep it. While perhaps an exaggeration, it makes the point that properly integrating the disciplines and underlying strategies of investment management, estate and philanthropic planning, risk management, governance and succession of a closely-held business, income tax planning and other considerations into a comprehensive plan and managing them on an ongoing basis is no easy task.

Perhaps a good place to start is an assessment of where you stand in implementing them. In that context and by way of a review of what we've discussed, I offer the following checklist.

Financial Independence

- You know where you stand regarding the capital required to sustain your desired lifestyle, after tax and inflation (i.e., what is "enough").
- You have sufficient liquidity to sustain yourself and your business during the "next" financial crisis.
- Your debt level is prudent.
- You have a plan to deploy surplus wealth for your family and society.

© The Author(s) 2019
R. P. Rojeck, *Wealth*,
https://doi.org/10.1007/978-3-030-24497-2_10

Vision and Values

- You have identified values that you wish to express and reinforce for the benefit of future generations and society.
- You have communicated your values and vision for family wealth in the context of your estate and philanthropic planning, inviting feedback from those affected.
- Your values are expressed in the structure of your documents and activities.

Involving the Next Generations

- You are preparing future generations to be effective stewards of family wealth.
- Your children and grandchildren are involved in managing and disbursing funds as part of your philanthropic activities.
- You have periodic family meetings or retreats to discuss matters relating to family governance and wealth management.
- You have considered using a family coach to facilitate discussions and help address challenging family dynamics, if necessary.

Estate Planning

- Your estate plan fosters a sense of opportunity, not merely providing an entitlement and encouraging a "shirtsleeves to shirtsleeves in three generations" outcome.
- You know what your federal estate tax liability is today and into the future based upon a forecast of estate growth.
- You have an active gifting plan taking full advantage of the annual exclusion, gift, estate, and generation skipping exemptions as well as valuation discount and "freeze" strategies.
- Your gifting plan seeks to remove assets from the transfer tax system, not merely shifting them down a generation.

Philanthropy

- You have determined how much wealth is enough for your family and, in turn, available to benefit society.

- Your charitable giving is focused as to causes and structured to encourage accountability and desired outcomes.
- You have incorporated charitable strategies in order to better achieve your wealth preservation and transfer goals (e.g. CRT, CLAT, TCLAT, conservation easement, private foundation).

Business Succession Planning (If a Business Owner)

- If you plan to keep your business in the family, you have identified and communicated your views regarding successor management.
- You are preparing future leaders to lead through training, experience and "opportunities to fail" (with adequate safeguards against catastrophic results).
- For a family business, your estate plan addresses the implications for "inside versus outside" children, including the concept of equitable versus fair distribution.
- Your business agreements are up to date as to asset values, terms and conditions, and tax considerations.
- If you have no partners or family involvement in your business, you have developed a viable exit strategy.
- You know what your business is worth and are taking steps to maximize its marketability, if your plan is to sell.

Asset Protection

- You have periodic risk exposure audits and P&C insurance coverage reviews.
- Business and investment activities are conducted in suitable, properly maintained business entities and trusts.
- The question "if I were to lose everything, how much would it cost to start over" has been used as a litmus test for your asset protection strategies.
- Your estate planning documents incorporate structures protecting assets from creditors, judgments, or divorce of future generations.

Life Insurance

- You regularly receive re-illustrations of your life insurance policies to confirm that premiums are adequate to sustain coverage.

- You have considered life insurance funding for your business agreements and existing policies are aligned as to amount, owner, beneficiary, and premium payor with the agreements.
- You have considered life insurance as a means of estate tax payment and existing policies are aligned as to amount, owner, beneficiary, and premium payor.

Investment Management

- Your investment portfolio is aligned with your risk tolerance, return objectives, and views on ESG issues. Portfolio management is guided by an Investment Policy Statement.
- Your portfolio activity is managed to minimize the impact of income taxes.
- You are minimizing portfolio expenses (e.g. advisory and portfolio manager fees, trading costs and mark-ups, custodial fees, etc.).
- Your active managers are adding value on a risk-adjusted basis (i.e. are providing a higher return and/or lower risk than their benchmark).
- You are satisfied with the performance of your investment portfolio, compared with a suitable benchmark.

Income Tax

- You are satisfied with the amount of income tax you are paying.
- You have considered available deferral strategies (e.g., "C" corporation with January 31st fiscal year).
- You have considered available income conversion strategies (e.g., changing state of legal residence).
- You have considered income diverting strategies (e.g., employing children or grandchildren in an unincorporated business).
- You have pursued available deductions (e.g., an oil and gas drilling investment).

How Did You Score?

I hope the above exercise was, at a minimum, thought-provoking. Perhaps it surfaced opportunities for improvement in your current planning. Most importantly, I hope it serves as a catalyst to helping you obtain the most from your advisory team and insuring that a qualified financial planning professional is a member of it.

Well, that's it! I hope you've found the reading of this book enjoyable, informative, and motivational. I wish you continued good fortune and enjoyment of the fruits of your success both for yourself, your family, and society.

Index

Made in United States
Orlando, FL
15 April 2024

45849760R00083

"*Wealth* is the most comprehensive such book I have ever read. It's applicable not just to the wealthy, but to their advisors as well."
—**Malin Burnham**, Former Chair, Burnham Real Estate Services; Former Vice-Chair, Cushman & Wakefield; San Diego Philanthropist and Civic Leader

"*Wealth* offers a fresh, holistic financial planning approach to meet the needs of today's wealthy. Wealth is an informative, easy-to-understand book for anyone who is looking to spend, grow and preserve their wealth."
—**Kevin Keller**, CEO, Certified Financial Planner Board of Standards, Inc.

"*Wealth* does a masterful job of guiding the reader through all the key wealth optimization issues, succinctly, but thoroughly. It's up-to-date, easy to digest, and motivates to action. Buy a copy for yourself...and another one for your advisor."
—**Tim Kochis**, JD, CFP®, CEO Kochis Global; Former CEO and Chair, Aspiriant; Former Chair, CFP Board of Standards

"*Wealth* offers clear, insightful, and much needed guidance to all of us who want to optimize financial assets in a manner that synchronizes personal goals and life aspirations."
—**Gail K. Naughton**, PhD, Founder, CEO, Histogen Inc.; Former Dean, College of Business Administration, San Diego State University, USA

"*Wealth* provokes you with the right questions and provides highly useful techniques and information to accomplish your goals. Its advice to integrate all aspects of growing and protecting your wealth is spot on."
—**G. Joseph Votava**, Jr., Esq., CPA, CEO Seneca Financial Advisors; Former Chair, Financial Planning Association; Former Chair, National Endowment for Financial Education

ISBN 978-3-030-24499-6

9 783030 244996

www.palgrave.com

palgrave
macmillan